Surviving Grief

By VICTORIA MITCHELL

NORTHAMPTON HOUSE PRESS

Acknowledgement is made for kind permission to reprint the following: *No Hard Feelings* Words and Music by Timothy Avett, Scott Avett and Bob Crawford. Copyright @ 2016 Ramseur Family Fold Music, First Big Snow Publishing, Nemoiv Music and Truth Comes True Publishing. All Rights Administered by BMG Rights Management (US) LLC. All Rights Reserved. Used by Permission. *Reprinted by Permission of Hal Leonard, LLC*

Front cover image by Niadra LLC.

ISBN 979-8-8690-7013-5 (Ingram print edition)

Library of Congress Control Number: 2023920397

Published by Northampton House Press, www.northampton-house.com. Franktown Virginia USA.

For those I love,

with me now and gone before.

Love is worth it.

CONTENTS

INTRODUCTION

There's nothing easy about grief. That includes writing a book about it. A focus on loss becomes an emotional journey for both reader and writer.

The decision to pen these pages opened my heart to all I might feel. I knew I needed to share my own stories for this to matter. If I hid behind statistics and research, how could I ask you to be vulnerable to your losses? I would teach you little if I didn't speak my own truth. With that truth, I offer a path to feel your grief, process your pain, and come to healing.

But why me? Who made me an expert? I feel presumptuous placing myself in that role by writing this book. Yes. I've known loss. Yes. I spent years as a therapist working with grieving clients. At the same time, I'm humbled every day by the vulnerability of others. I'm often brought to tears while reading accounts of struggles with loss and tragedy. So, it's with humility I take on this task. I offer you my inadequacy and my expertise. Why me? I guess the answer is, why not me?

Now in my seventies, I've lived a lot, loved much, and lost many. I'll share with an open heart, and we'll get through this together.

On the eve of his January 2021 inauguration, President Joe Biden spoke at a memorial for those lost to Covid-19. Four hundred luminaries were lit, to honor the, then, 400,000 Americans who had died. The luminaries lined the Lincoln Memorial reflecting pool as the Washington Memorial backlit the night sky. He said, "To heal, we must remember. It's hard, sometimes, to remember. But that's how we heal."[1] A simple statement of great truth from a man who's known immense loss. It's in the telling of stories, of remembering, of sharing our sorrow that we move forward.

Grief is universal. It's also deeply personal. But grief, like love, needs to be shared. The story becomes a valuable healing tool. To know others survive, that smiles reappear, that life can be good again – that's the best therapy. I made it through. You will as well.

We'll talk of healing. The word implies restoration to a previous level of function, of wellness, of health. Recovering from grief is different. It changes you. Things will never go back to exactly how they were. Your experience becomes a part of you. You carry it with you. But you can't go back.

Surviving Grief is part professional and more memoir, as I travel between my years of practice and the lessons of my life. Some events of my story are tragic. Some may seem benign. Our history defines how we view and experience loss. You'll have moments of sorrow that others won't understand. But they're important to you. As you move along in the telling of your story, memories will surface. They'll make you sad. We're here to honor all of them. They build and intertwine throughout your life, creating the helix of your heart.

Grief, sorrow, loss, mourning – they're anything but neat and orderly. Nor are they universal in their manifestation and expression. Grief is messy, chaotic, unpredictable, and tortuous. It's heart shattering and soul searing. As you come with me on this journey, you'll find glimpses of insight, random thoughts, quick changes of direction, and moments of hesitance. There's too much feeling to be wrapped in a neat package. We'll forge a path through confusion, contradiction, and confoundedness. And through this process we'll let anguish transcend to beauty, sorrow to joy, and panic to peace.

We'll walk through the agony that accompanies new loss. We'll share moments of sorrow that surprise us for months and years, throwing us off balance without warning. It might be the body wash scent that lingers in the shower, the Tums found in the drawer of the bedside table, the Constant Comment tea bags in the back of the cabinet, the spring bloom of a purple bearded iris planted the year before – blasts of instant sorrow that hit at the most unexpected times. We'll work on methods to get through these tearful tugs, permitting them to bring memories and loving thoughts to a sorrowful heart, as we walk and sometimes crawl that shadowed path.

In the first chapters, we'll look at grief from different directions - its paradoxes, contradictions, and truths. We'll explore cultural and societal perspectives that influence how we respond to loss.

But getting through the sorrow is what we're here for. We'll primarily address loss of loved ones. We'll also honor the pricks of pain that still come when we remember our beloved pet, a failed promotion, a home we left behind. It could be the soft memory of a worn stuffed rabbit lost in the lake when you were five. It could be a blankie. It could be your first goldfish. Or it could be the death of the person you love more than anything in this world. It's the honoring of what each of these meant. It's the memories of having them and losing them. It's the certainty that their presence shaped you and is woven into your being.

Later chapters will address loss of relationship, surviving holidays, complicated grief, and children's grief. We'll also look at spiritual impacts and how to help others who experience loss. We'll speak to life changes. And contemplate how we'll face our own death and the legacy we wish to leave. How do you hope to say good-bye? How do you want to be remembered?

Finally, we'll focus directly on healing as we create a toolbox for, first surviving, then coping and moving forward in an altered world. What will moving forward look like? What will you bring with you? Your heart will find the means to hold your loss in such a way that your life grows around it. It becomes a part of you, as surely as the oxygen you breathe.

In each section, you'll find brief, informal assignments and writing prompts. These will offer insights as you process your feelings. I suggest you get a notebook. I'm partial to beautiful things so I'd recommend a blank journal in your favorite color that feels soft to your hand. Also, a special pen. I like a fountain pen, but whatever you like. If these aren't available to you, any loose-leaf paper, spiral notebook or roll of paper towels will do. It's your reflections that are important. They'll start as only notes. There isn't a definite chronology to these prompts, so it'll feel disorganized at first. But what you write will build a testament to what you've loved in your life, a legacy left for you. As you continue, your grief story will emerge. At the conclusion of *Surviving Grief,* you'll find a summary of the writing prompts in Appendix B.

In the three-plus years it's taken to write this book, new sorrow has befallen us on a personal, communal, and global level. It began to feel like I could add new sorrow every day that I wrote. While I planned to address national grief, I never would've imagined the perspective gained from these past years of isolation, lifestyle change, and loss. Little did I know, as 2019 turned to 2020 and beyond, the entire globe would enter a crisis - the COVID-19 pandemic.

The sorrow and trauma are still unfolding. As the Midwest spring bloomed, years beyond the "two-week shutdown" that turned to months, there were hopeful signs. Yet, even as I wrote those last words, my husband and I tested positive for COVID. Even with vaccines and boosters, we were mildly ill and exhausted. I thanked God, the universe, and my cautious self for the precautions we took in the early days - when a positive test might have been a death sentence.

Neither could I have predicted how personal the chapter on loss of self would become. A new perspective emerged as I walked through my own cancer journey. That story has a happy ending, but I'm still processing how it's changed my self-view and how I greet each day.

I was a psychotherapist for thirty-plus years and a psychiatric nurse prior to that. I learned early that part of going on after loss is making good come from the sorrow. Healing my own losses led to a focus on grief work. Following the late-term stillbirth of our son, I found myself serving those with reproductive grief issues – infertility, miscarriage, stillbirth, neonatal loss, and abortion.

Over the years, I wrote magazine essays, poems, and op-eds on mental health topics – many about grief. You'll find several of these historically contextual essays and poems in Appendix A. After retirement I wrote my first book, *Happiness Calling: A Practical Guide for Saying Yes to Life's Joy.* In it I shared what I learned in my practice about the struggle to find joy. Grief is one of the darkest clouds that block our vison of happiness. If you've read that volume, some of the tools and exercises here will seem familiar. After all, the final task of healing from loss is allowing happiness to find you once more.

This book doesn't provide psychological services, and I am not acting in a professional capacity. I've included advice about how to find a therapist or support group, should you choose to seek professional help.

Instead, my goal is to provide a resource for your healing, learning, and exploration. Anecdotes, case references, and examples herein are a compilation of my experiences and those of others, as well as a very modest degree of creative license. Some proper names and identifying details have been changed to protect the privacy of individuals.

Throughout the text, I offer theories and thoughts about

anguish and loss. Some are based on research, and for those I provide references. Others come from the biases and beliefs of a stubborn, opinionated old therapist, forged over decades. My former colleagues and employers may not always agree with these, but they've served me and my clients well. I hope you find them meaningful and useful.

These pages reflect my way of grieving, my perceptions of how it feels and how I work through loss. You and I may suffer differently – depending on genetic, family, gender, and cultural factors. You may be quieter, less inclined to talk about your loss. Or you may be culturally more expressive. Knowing yourself and what's best for you is an important tool in working through any challenge. There is no right or wrong way to grieve. However, there can be roadblocks and detours along your path that make it harder and more complicated. We'll address these and how to navigate through what might get in your way.

As we move forward, the comingling of happiness and sorrow becomes poignantly clear. The connection of deep polar emotions is often noted.

Kahlil Gibran wrote in *The Prophet*, "Your joy is your sorrow unmasked. And the selfsame well from which your laughter rises was oftentimes filled with your tears…. The deeper that sorrow carves into your being, the more joy you can contain." [2] We can't know joy without experiencing sorrow. Each is a light unto the other.

If we have love, we have loss. Loss of life. Loss of self. Loss of dreams. When we lose what makes us happy, we feel grief. It's a thief of joy yet can also become a gateway to tender self-discovery. We'll see how it looks, feels, sounds, and smells. Our grief stories live in us and change us. We're here to honor those stories and find strength that sustains.

It's been said that without grief and pain, no one can develop into a fully human being. Every loss is an opportunity to grow. To grow deeper and more in tune with everyone who suffers – which is every one of us.

I want to help create a path for your pain. To help you see the first glimpses of light and engender hope that life will go on. Most of all, I want to help you find the means to carry your loved one in your heart. In doing so, you'll not only survive loss, but you'll experience a softness and compassion that only walking through this valley can offer.

This is a book of love.
This is a book of loss.
This is a book of hope.
This is a book of healing.

PART I: OUR SOCIETY AND GRIEF

We begin our journey by looking at societal perspectives of death, at loss and grief in the arts, and at our own unconscious patterns. These are subtle messages and unspoken rules from where we live, how we're raised, what we read, what we think, and what we believe. They teach us how to grieve. They define our vulnerability, especially if we experience early loss. They shape our rituals, our fear, our shame, our pride. Our culture and our history tell us what is appropriate and what to hide. It shapes our relationship with death and dying.

Communal denial

When someone dies in America, Britain, Canada, and many other lands, we use euphemisms to frame it. They've passed on, passed away, went home, transitioned. He went to a better place, or to the eternal sleep, or to heaven. She crossed over, passed through the veil, had her homecoming, or crossed the rainbow bridge.

In a scene from the movie *Patch Adams*, Robin Williams goes further with "To push up posies. To become extinct. Curtains, deceased, demised, departed, and defunct." He asks later, "What's wrong with death, sir? What are we so mortally afraid of? Why can't we treat death with a certain amount of humanity, and dignity, and decency?" [3]

It's as if the word for the most natural guaranteed event of the human experience can't be said aloud. It must be buffered, diluted, made more palatable. We're born. We live. We die. It's a simple equation.

On the surface, it doesn't give the slightest hint of the pain that final step creates. But we all know. And we'd all like to avoid it.

The certainty that our loved ones will die, that we'll die, leads us to a strong denial system. We cloak ourselves and those we hold close in an imagined suit of armor – our protection from the reality of human frailty, and the truth of how much it'll hurt. Then someone we love dies. Our protection is gone. Anguish overwhelms. We're at our most vulnerable, like a turtle without a shell. Every thought and every feeling hurts.

We struggle to understand. Does it make us grieve less, carry less sorrow if we pretend actual death doesn't exist? I haven't found that to be the case. This person or pup I loved with all my heart has left this earth. It doesn't matter if they crossed over, passed on, or went to be with God. They're gone, and I'm hurting. And as much as my control-addicted brain wants to make sense of it, I never will.

A beautiful quote from an unknown source notes that "Most fears in life trace back to fear of death. But death isn't something to fear or hide. It's as natural as birth, a beautiful exhale, a return to soil to seed new life. We only fear what we refuse to see. With acceptance comes peace." [4]

Author Margaret Rinkl, in a guest essay for *The New York Times*, wonders at others' inability to honor grief. "We talk of 'processing' loss, or reckoning with it and moving on, as though bright life could not possibly include an unvanquishable darkness. Our culture persists in treating mourning as an unpleasant process we are obliged to endure while waiting for real life to restore itself." [5]

Buddhist teachings instruct us to live with an awareness of life's impermanence. We're not good at that. We cling to flashes of bliss, grip great moments, and savor the sweetest of times. We rationally understand that nothing lasts forever. But we shy from the reality. It's difficult to grasp that this moment, kiss, or chocolate won't last. Much less life.

Pema Chodron, in *How We Live is How We Die*, shares that, during retreats, this chant is recited: "Like a shooting star, a visual fault, a candle flame, an illusion, a dewdrop, a water bubble, a dream, lightning, a cloud: regard conditional dharmas like that. This verse is meant to impress impermanence on our minds so we can get used to its presence in our lives." [6]

What if we were able to embrace the impermanence, honoring the constant state of flow? Could it help us live better and love better during our earthly experience? Could that help us heal after loss? If we embraced this truth, we'd face that, at any given second, this earthly life may end. In facing this reality, we could avoid many of the torturing "what ifs" and "why didn't I's" that come after loss. If we were able to live life appreciating every minute as potentially our last, we would be more sensitive to ours and the needs of others. We'd give ourselves freely to those we love and those in need of kindness. We'd notice more. We'd listen more. We'd love more.

I'm aware that if I know someone is near the end of their life, I'm more tender, more loving, gentler. Whether it be my grandmother or an aging pet, I talk to them more, touch them more, listen more. I say the heartfelt words I want them to hear. I give them my time. What if I did that with everyone in my life circle? So much regret and guilt that holds on to grief's pantlegs could be released. Could that be helpful in our healing?

It could. But carrying the burden of that constant awareness is too heavy for our daily consciousness. Our heart isn't wired to live that close to the flame of life's fragility. There is self-protection in our denial after all.

Take a minute with your journal to think about a time when you knew someone was going to die. How were you different? How did you feel about it? Do you think it changed how you grieved in any way?

All living things die at the end of their earthly journey. On that same journey, the heart is pulled toward love, connection, attachment. Why do the most natural elements of life – love and death – lead to such pain when they, inevitably, collide – when one is sacrificed to the other?

In my therapy practice, I met people who said they avoided loving anything because it would just die. Their world view assumed abandonment, anticipating the hurt of loss. This was hard reasoning to challenge because I couldn't guarantee that if they risked opening their heart, they wouldn't be hurt. All I could do was help them to healing so they could experience the preciousness of loving and being loved. In a way, they were right. We take a risk when we love - when we give someone or something our heart. But it's also what gives life meaning. Loving our lover, our family, our neighbors, our friends. Joy lives there. Without connections, we're left with emptiness. And what kind of life is that?

It's a challenge to understand the contradiction, why our greatest joy leads to our greatest pain. but it mustn't stop us from loving and connecting. Every person who touches our life, no matter how long, has some impact on who we are. Every connection, every experience teaches us something – even loss. Maybe especially loss.

To live a full life, we accept the risk. We become willing to pay the ultimate price for the joy of loving. Grief is the cost of love.

Tallu Schuyler Quinn, in her dying memoir, *What We Wish Were True,* reflects that "unimaginable suffering and deep love are two sides of the same coin." [7]

In an Instagram post, Elizabeth Gilbert wrote, "Grief does not obey your plans, or your wishes. Grief will do whatever it wants to you, whenever it wants to. In that regard, grief has a lot in common with love." [8]

Our brain tries to make sense of this whole mystery. But if we accept the contradiction, letting it teach us the subtleties of life that defy rational cognition, we may find something beautiful. On this earthbound plane we're limited in our understanding. I believe each of us will have a lovely "aha" moment when we die. And, once we're there, it likely won't matter to us anymore.

Grief and the arts

Earlier, I mentioned the arts. America has a death phobia, while paradoxically watching television and movie deaths each and every day. Perhaps that's part of our attempt to come to terms with mortality.

We've wrestled with death's power throughout history. Mythology, fables, fairytales feature tragedy and loss. It's in our literature, movies, plays, operas, ballets, and songs. When my children first started watching Disney movies, I was struck by how often someone dies – a parent, or a pet, or the kind gentleman next door. It seemed to me that way too often it was the mother.

Often, the writer of the book or the movie or the lyrics is using their creative gift as a tool to process their own grief. It's what we do. We tell our stories – to find a place to put it, to make good come from it. Their works allow the readers and viewers, to work through our own sorrow as we cry at their movies and weep over their books and sad songs. It creates an outlet for our own soulful melancholy. We cry for Bambi and Little Foot. We wring our hands at Mimi's deathbed in Puccini's *La Boheme.* We cry like babies when Old Yeller goes down, and we tearfully sing "The Last Kiss" as if it were our own.

Classics old and new echo with grief. Harry Potter faced a life of multiple losses and chronic grief, which played a pivotal role in his actions at Hogwarts and beyond. Every soap opera – daytime and primetime – has at least one story line of loss and healing going on. Historical dramas like *Downton Abbey* have characters gone too soon. For any *Gray's Anatomy* fan, the term "007" takes on a whole new meaning. Ask any man over sixty if he cried watching *Brian's Song*, or any teen who watched *The Fault of our Stars*, or any mother watching *Stepmom*. I predict each would describe the movie as sad and painful and cathartic. And, yes, they'd watch it again!

While writing her book *Atlas of the Heart*, Brene' Brown sought social media input on favorite sad movies. She received over a hundred thousand responses. The list included: *"Life is Beautiful, Terms of Endearment, Beaches, The Joy Luck Club, The Color Purple, Steel Magnolias, Brokeback Mountain, P.S. I Love You, Inside Out, Up,* and every movie made where a dog dies." [9]

Listen to Leonard Cohen's, Johnny Cash's, and Warren Zevon's last albums. Your heart will be pulled in as their words pay homage to their end-of-life thoughts– testaments to how they mourned their impending deaths.

One of the most profound recent quotes from the arts, comes from Taylor Sheridan's poignantly beautiful narrative in the television series *1883*. A dying young woman wonders "What is death? What is this thing we all share? Rabbits, birds, horses, trees. Everyone I love and everyone who loves me. Even stars die. And we know absolutely nothing of it."[10] How do we come to accept death as a natural part of the great circle of life, when we have so little understanding? Coming to terms with this great mystery is everyone's personal journey of tears.

Art and literature give us opportunities to cry for our own losses through these stories and songs. An event, book, movie may feel devastating, while others around you don't seem affected. If that occurs, look to your memories. You'll find a connection to some loss in your history that makes those feelings more intense. By knowing your story and unique vulnerability, you can take time to honor what you find in these circumstances.

Spend a few minutes now to reflect. Think about what movies or books or songs stand out in your heart. What scenes or lyrics immediately bring a burning rush of tears? Then think about why. Write about this "why" in your journal.

In *Happiness Calling* I related a story of a young woman watching a movie with friends. A scene of a young girl being taken from her mother by a child welfare worker brought tears overflowing to the point of sobs. Then she noticed that no one else was crying. Thinking about it later, she realized that scene had triggered her early memories of her mom's constant threats of abandonment – living in terror of being sent away if she wasn't "good." She'd carried this chronic sorrow into adulthood. Getting in touch with these feelings explained her emotionality during the movie and was a breakthrough in her therapy.

My own story includes a visceral response to the 1970's version of *A Star is Born*. I watched Kris Kristofferson's character speed off in his shiny sports car down a dusty desert road to end his life. This was a few months after my father died in an auto accident. (You'll read that story in a later chapter.) Unprepared for the movie scene, I felt faint as I cried and cried while others dabbed away a couple tears.

There's meaning in our emotions, especially those we're unprepared for, the ones that take our breath way or make the room spin. Follow that thread that has temporarily unraveled from your life force. It'll lead you to a deeper connection.

Sorrow is always to be trusted. We find different emotional spaces to put our pain. When we experience a new loss, there's a bit of every previous grief that attaches itself to it, like metal shavings to a magnet.

Quantifying grief

In an ideal world, there wouldn't be any quantifying of grief. There's no hierarchy - no scale to weigh how much you grieve in any certain situation or how much one loss means more than another. We do have cultural assumptions, though. We view loss of a younger person as tragic. If someone's aged, it's easier to assume grief should be reduced. That loved one lived a long full life, after all, and may even seem ready to let go.

These assumptions aren't universally correct. My grief story holds space for the death of my stepfather. He was there four more years than my dad, so the term stepfather seems like a misnomer. My mother married him two years after Dad died. He went through all the hard stuff of her early widowhood. Neither she, nor I, would have made it through without him.

He was a fifty-one-year-old churchgoing, pipe smoking, grade school principal, bachelor. Studious and prone to contemplation, he was the opposite of my dad in personality. He likely never tasted whiskey and certainly never got in a fight, or bet on horses, or taught children to play craps on Sunday mornings. He did tend to view us with a more critical eye than my dad, who was always easy going. But they had one thing in common - they were both really good guys with big hearts, who loved my mama.

My stepdad and Mom retired to Florida, where several of his siblings lived, and spent summers in Illinois. When she became ill, they came back here permanently, initially in a nursing home, then to our home, and finally to an apartment. He was a constant support and caregiver. The only thing I faulted him for was donating all my mother's things within days of her funeral because he couldn't bear the reminders.

After her death, he made it through one more Illinois winter before he decided to return to Florida. We understood. He was eighty, relatively healthy, walked three miles a day and remained socially and intellectually active. He found an apartment, packed a moving van, transferred his mail, and was staying at our house for three days until he and his brother would drive to Florida.

Then he hurt his toe. This led to a cascade of medical mistakes that toppled like dominoes ending in his death a week later. The night he died he talked me into going home because the next day was the first day of school for his beloved grandchildren. I was awakened by a phone call at 1:30 am telling me he had fallen and wasn't responsive. This translated to falling out of bed because no one answered his call light to use the bathroom, and his life-sustaining high pressure oxygen mask had wrenched from his face as he fell. His death, while he was eighty, and had lived a good life, was a tragedy. Reading his obituary one would never know that. Anyone who knew him understood he had been robbed of many years.

Some losses feel more tragic and traumatic than others, but does it translate into a deeper grief? Should it be easier if the loss is expected? Does the young mother whose husband dies in an accident grieve more than an eighty-year-old who lost his wife of sixty years to cancer? Will they face different challenges as life moves on? Yes. Will their healing look different? Yes.

But no one can predict the scope and depth of personal grief.

It depends on what we lose, and our history. One of my clients was engaged to her high school sweetheart. He died in a farm accident weeks before their wedding. Her grief was crippling. Her healing was slow. Her grief history was one of early loss of her father. She went on to have a good life, but never married. The inherent risk that commitment carried was too much for her. Yet another young woman may suffer a similar loss and be able to go on and find love and marriage. How can we say that one grieved more deeply than the other?

How do you view the death of a homeless person compared to a father of three? How do you compare the death of a murderer with that of a heart surgeon? How do you feel if you see a dog or cat lying dead on the side of the road as opposed to a possum or raccoon? For years, as a pescatarian, I chose the animals my conscience wouldn't let me eat. The fish wasn't one of them. What if someone morbidly obese dies? What if a person dies while driving intoxicated or is shot confronting police? We make flash judgements about how sad or tragic a situation is.

We even tend to quantify our own emotions. If we miscarry a pregnancy, there's grief, but when we think about a mother who lost a toddler, we may feel our grief isn't valid, leaving it disenfranchised.

There's a subtle judge and jury in the recesses of our brains with opinions on who deserves to die and who deserves to be grieved. It's a dark side of our nature. It's helpful to understand and face these snap judgements. Being aware of our biases and prejudices helps us to manage them and what comes out of our mouth, especially if someone needs comfort.

We never know another person's heart and we don't know their story unless they choose to tell us. Respect others' grieving. Don't judge it based on your standards of appropriateness. If we open our hearts, rather than our quick to judge brain, we'll reach new levels of empathy and connection. No matter what the circumstance, somebody or something was loved and now they're gone. And a broken heart grieves.

Grief's privilege

Societal realities also dictate how some "should" recover from loss or view grief. For most of this book we look at the "norms" of how and how long we grieve. But there's an unspoken privilege to be able to do that.

There are those among us who, literally, can't afford to grieve. The mere survival needs of a family may short circuit the mourning process. Many rituals aren't available to those of lower socio-economic status due to prohibitive costs.

The same can be said about care and support after loss. The cost may make it impossible to access care. There may also be issues of transportation availability and even lack of knowledge that these care options exist.

In an essay, Emma Payne wrote "Waiting lists, hourly rates, geography and cultural distrust make grief support inaccessible for many Americans."[11]

She goes on to say she "looks forward to the day when grief support will be available to everyone who needs it. Employers, policy makers, practitioners, and insurers all have a role to play." [12]

Take time with your journal before moving on to Part II. Look at your perceptions of loss and what quantifiers you carry. I think a mass murderer of babies deserved to die, and a drunk boater who caused the death of five good people shouldn't have survived. There are more judgements I carry in my heart, but these two are recent and fresh. This is an important journal entry. Acknowledging your inclination to judge is valuable. You may find a new level of empathy developing and a greater capacity for acceptance.

PART II: SO MUCH SADNESS

No matter how we balance our mental scales of justice, when someone we love dies, we're lost. There isn't time for critical thought when we're trying to survive. It's feelings. All feelings.

The sweater

There's this old pea-green wool sweater. It's threadbare with frayed sleeves and several holes down by the belly button area. I've developed an allergy to wool so I can't wear it anymore, though I still try to, now and then. My nose starts to itch and my neck flushes whenever I lean in to sniff a remnant of Old Spice, wintergreen mints, and cement dust.

After forty-seven years, this moth-nibbled sweater is what I have left of my dad. Oh, there's the worn-out shadow box with cuff links and an ID bracelet he gave to Mom when he was seventeen, a vintage bottle opener given out as a company Christmas gift one year, and a toy cement truck from somewhere. And there's the picture album of faded black and whites. I value these shreds of his life, but they never went over his head or touched his skin. Only the sweater.

I don't know if the sweater has any of his smell left, but my brain says it does. My neural pathways tell me that my daddy still lives on – in smells, memories, spirit. Wishful thinking? Who knows? Who cares? For those few minutes, itchy nose, and all, I get to feel hugged by him. I get to lay my head against his chest. I get to remember. And I get to shed tears. This reunion with the sweater doesn't happen much anymore. Life has gone on. It now takes a special holiday memory, or a once-shared song, or a newborn grandson's cleft chin to send me to the sweater, and back to my young adult self. My grief has been proclaimed healed for many decades. But that doesn't mean it's gone. It lies beneath the surface of accumulated life, a fiber woven into the multitude of sorrow and joy that shades and colors my being, shaping my heart.

I share the sweater story as a model of what healing from grief looks like. We heal but will still be tweaked by sadness on occasion. I want to help you heal. But I can't delete sorrow from your life, any more than you would want precious memories erased from your heart. That's the truth of healing. It's bittersweet news, but with flashes of grief that hit years after loss, there are also soft smiles and sweet reminiscences tucked into your heart. It's as if the death of a loved one shakes us so that our grieving soul is somehow catapulted to right beneath the skin, pulsating in the flow of our blood and the catch of our breath. Once released, it can't be resealed into the depth of our spirit. It lives in our nerve endings and can be reawakened at any time, danced into the rhythm of our heartbeat again by a song, a feel, or touch.

Poet Ranata Suzuki wrote, "I never knew the aftermath would be this painful. I never knew that you miss someone with the same fervor with which you loved them."[13]

In *The Year of Magical Thinking* Joan Didion said, "Grief is different. Grief has no distance. Grief comes in waves, paroxysms, sudden apprehensions that weaken the knees and blind the eyes and obliterate the dailiness of life."[14]

In the online magazine *Slate*, psychologist Sherry Walling wrote about her brother's suicide and how it impacted her practice. She writes, "You don't recover from grief. You integrate it. It doesn't leave you. It gets absorbed into you until it's a part of what makes you whole."[15]

This truth was a professional challenge in my early years of practice – this inability to take all the pain away. I chose my profession to help others find peace, contentment, joy. As I walked with clients through the agony of loss, it took constant adjustment of expectation. It hurt to fall short of "making it all better." As a clinician, I understood the process of working through loss, but it often left me helpless as I dealt with how long it took. There are no immediate answers for a tearful widow who just found the anniversary card her husband bought, but never got to give her. There is no quick comfort for a mother who found her dead son's favorite sweatshirt in the car trunk, still smelling of his last basketball game. There are only tears for the young father of three babies recently diagnosed with terminal cancer. I was able to promise it would get better, but I couldn't tell a hurting soul that it'll go away and never touch them again.

So, I listened and held hands. I cried with them and handed over tissues as they shared photos and stories of their person. I held their lost dreams. I sensed when they needed stillness and when they waited for a little push. I knew the dark, winding path of unknowns that lay ahead. I wanted to save them from it, to bypass it, to "get out of jail" free. I wanted to give them lightness and laughter. But all I could do was walk alongside and promise that one day they would feel sunshine, appreciate a breeze, and laugh from the bottom of the belly once more – with the occasional storm of breakthrough sorrow.

As I became more focused on loss and grief, I turned to psychiatrist, Elizabeth Kubler-Ross's ground-breaking work. The death of her pet rabbit, Blackie, led to her eventual dedication to her research. She outlined the stages of grief for the dying and the survivors. Her book *On Death and Dying* identified these stages as first denial, as the brain blocks the unimaginable, and on to anger as one struggles with why me. The next stage is bargaining seeking deals with God. She identifies the next stage as depression. Reality sets in and we're faced with our own death or that of a loved one. The final stage is acceptance, often a quiet recognition that this is all real. Initially, these stages were thought to be linear, one after another – on to acceptance. But it became clear that each one is passed in and out of many times. While there have been challenges to her model and identification of other stages, I found her observations to be an invaluable tool in my own work with clients. You'll find her ideas scattered throughout these pages. [16]

In my (and likely yours) wishful interpretation of Kubler-Ross's work, we still yearn to think that the progression through the stages is a straight line. Get to resolution and you're done. I wish it were like that, but it's not. I yearned for a "here's the facts and here's what to do about it" manual. But that would be good for my head, bad for my heart. It would be nice to keep grief clean and organized. It would be easier to navigate if it was a dot-to-dot journey of denial, anger, bargaining, depression, acceptance, and done. I'd love to give you a step-by-step way out of suffering. But it wouldn't be truth.

As Kubler-Ross emphasized, there's no predictable pattern in the journey. In the end, it's the rhythm of your own loss and healing that dictates your path. Her book does, however, act as a guide and a way to feel a bit of control over the often out of control feelings of early grief. Being aware of the stages helps steady us when we feel as if we're falling down the chute of bargains and denial. There is a season for unrelenting pain, anger, bargains, and resolution. As the seasons overlap and fold into each other you'll eventually find a purpose, a meaning. Some call this the sixth stage of grief.

Before moving on, take a few minutes to focus on how you're feeling right now in reference to Kubler-Ross's stages. Don't go beyond the now – not backward or ahead. This morning you may have felt different. But it's the right now that matters. Think about the stages – denial, anger, bargaining, depression, acceptance. Where are you? Journal a note. Until you're done with this book, and beyond should you choose, take a minute at the end of each day. Think about where you are and write it in your notebook. Another step in chronicling your journey – your grief story.

Loss

Loss creates sorrow. Say the word "sorrow" to yourself. It's onomatopoetic. See how it sits on your tongue, your lips. "Sorrow." "Oh." "Oh no." As you say it, you feel the pull downward – away from sunlight, away from laughter.

Loss creates anguish. Ranata Suzuki writes that it's another "one of those words you understand the meaning of just by the way that it sounds. It has this gnarling rasp to it as you twist your mouth around to say it…kind of like what feeling it does to your insides. It's an awful, drawn out, knotted up word. It's also one of the things I feel without you." [17]

When we lose a loved one, we experience anguish so immense it leaves us in a heap on the floor. Overwhelmed, we wonder how we'll go on. How we'll get through even a second of this pain, much less a lifetime of it.

Sherry Walling states in her essay, "In my early grief the term heartache became literal. Going to work and parenting my children became physical challenges. I ached."[18]

Clients often walked through my door in this kind of pain - without hope, brought to their knees. My first task was to communicate unequivocal, unwavering faith that they could get through the suffering. I gave them my hope as a lifeline until they found their own. If you're drowning in a recent loss, let me offer you the same faith. The return to strength takes time. At first, it's a matter of holding on and letting others carry you. I promise that you'll find your legs again and stand strong to continue the journey.

But I'm not going to lie to you. The story of my dad's sweater tells you the greatest grief truth.

Like a serious wound to the body, your heart may be healing, yet at times it feels like you aren't. Loss is like shrapnel wound scars that will flare at unexpected moments. In *A Grief Observed*, CS Lewis recounts the aftermath of his wife's death. He reflects on days when things seem better and he's going to get along okay, "But then comes a red-hot memory and all this 'commonsense' vanishes like an ant in the mouth of a furnace."[19]

Once these flashes swing open that furnace door to your grief, the feelings rise. You're floating peacefully on calm water and are suddenly pulled under and held there until every cell is saturated with sorrow again. Defenses collapse under the pressure of this anguish. But then, you're released and rise back to the surface. And you go on. I experienced one of these moments while looking out my kitchen window. In a Midwest spring the redbud tree births exquisite purple flowers for about two weeks. I enjoy every minute. But this one morning, no good explanation why, I remembered my pregnant fantasy of holding my newborn and showing him the redbud tree from the window of his nursery. For some reason, the memory smacked me in a soft spot, and the feelings came rushing at me. I cried hard for about five minutes for my son who should be thirty-one. Then it cleared, and I went on with a softened heart for the day.

The first days

The immediate impact, the shock, the numbness, the pain does feel like drowning. It's a split second that changes everything. It's the undertow, pulling us under, the panic that life is about to end. We can't breathe, can't get air, can't find a place to land. It's like that – those first days. How do we keep from drowning then? It's others who must hold our head above water, giving us moments of respite. We let others grab us by the collar, or throw a life preserver from the pier. It's the lifeguard catching us in a strong grasp and hauling us to the shore. These rescuers take on many faces and shapes. It's the folks who come to wait for news with you; the ones holding vigil in the yard; the town and community who rescues and passes the word. It's the women with soap suds hands and boxes of Kleenex. It smells of fresh baked hams and apple pies and the constant fresh pot of coffee.

The first days feel alien. You're struggling in an alternate reality. A life that felt routine and predictable, in a blink of an eye, becomes surreal and macabre'.

There may be only one thing in your control - how you breathe. Like a spinning ballerina who holds a focal point to keep from falling, focus on your breath. Yes. if we're alive we breathe. But in times of fear, anxiety, stress, we tend to hold our breath, sucking air rapidly with shallow inhales and exhales. We use our shoulders rather than our diaphragm to move air, very inefficiently, in and out of our lungs. But shallow breathing doesn't allow for complete air exchange. The balance of oxygen and carbon dioxide can be disrupted, leaving us light-headed. It can lead to hyperventilation and fainting, not helpful in moving through the initial space of loss. So, pay attention to your breathing. Focus on the in and out, the expanding of your chest, feeling the air in the back of your throat, the softness of your palate, the contracting of your abdomen. Create a cadence of an in-out count. Hold on to this focus for dear life. It will help you feel more physically grounded.

In these early days, get through the basic activities of daily living. Sleep when it's time to. Eat when it's mealtime. You'll feel like a robot, but your brain needs routine as it tries to make sense of the shock. Shower. Change clothes. Brush your teeth. If you've not experienced loss, this may sound ludicrous. If you've been through it, you know what I mean. It's these mechanical proofs of life that keep us moving forward.

Which is worse – knowing death is coming or unexpected loss? My mom, whose husband died in an auto accident, and her friend whose husband died a slow death from cancer tearfully discussed this at my dad's visitation. I've experienced both. The early stages of grief are impacted a great deal by these two scenarios – sudden loss or one we're prepared for.

Tallu Schuyler Quinn spoke of this as she prepared for her own death. "A lot of people die unexpectedly, and tragically there is no time for them or their loved ones to process what they will lose but haven't lost yet. I have thought often about how difficult it is to have a terminal illness, but what a gift it is to have this time to do my best to align my days with what is important to me." [20]

In her *New York Times* guest essay, Margaret Renkl speaks of the difference as her father had a long illness and her mother died suddenly. "Even in the midst of calamitous grief, I understood the difference: My father's long illness had given me time to work death into the daily patterns of my life. My mother's sudden death had obliterated any illusion that daily patterns are trustworthy."[21]

With sudden loss, we're dealing with the anguish of saying good-bye. But we're also blasted with the shock of the unexpected trauma that comes with that. The brain goes into survival mode, trying to make sense of the unthinkable. We're thrown into that haze of unreality.

When a loved one has been ill for some time, some grief work occurs before their death. Perhaps you'll get to say good-bye, talk about what needs talked about, make plans to have your loved one's wishes carried out for funerals, memorials, obituaries. It may be made more difficult near the end if there's suffering and pain. There may even be relief when you know they're at peace. But you got to hold their hand - to say the words you wanted to say and they wanted to hear. You got to lay your head on their chest. You got to say good-bye.

Jason Isbell, in his song "If We Were Vampires," speaks to the reality that he and his partner will not live forever, and one of them will be alone one day. He recognizes that he treats his partner gentler knowing their time may be short.[22]

On her Instagram, @lesliechill, Leslie Hill chronicled the months that led to her husband Jeff's death from terminal cancer. In pictures with few words, she offered the beauty and sorrow of moments they shared with each other and the village of support that surrounded them. Even as his health declined, they did their best to live in love and connection. Today, Leslie continues to be surrounded by her friends as she carries her memories of Jeff and their life together into her future. Hers is a lovely story of being fully present as her partner spent his last days, sharing as much as she possibly could.[23]

Unexpected death leaves you with none of that. He's here. Then He's gone. Her cup of coffee may still be warm. His pajamas might be on the bedroom floor. Her towel may still be damp from her shower. Your cheek may still feel a little chafe from his whiskered kiss. But he's gone.

When the Oklahoma City bombing occurred in 1995, precious babies died. One heartbroken mama still had powdered sugar on her cheek from her boys' breakfast donut kisses when she saw the building explode and collapse onto their childcare center.

They're there. Then they aren't.

A blink of an eye. A split second.

As the brain tries to regain some traction, tries to find that footing in a spinning world – you're called to make plans, pick out suits, go through pictures, make financial decisions, select songs, flowers, caskets, urns. You're expected to shower and dress, to greet people appropriately without shrieking. All this as the brain is still groping. Did this happen? Is it real? Is this a bad dream? When will I wake up? But you are awake and walking through a silver-hazed veil that protects your psyche until, slowly, reality comes into its nightmare of focus.

Yes. The immediate phase is different for these two situations-sudden or expected. From that point, though, once the brain's found its course, the grief we experience, no matter what the circumstances is eerily similar, while uniquely personal. In the end after the formalities and the gatherings and letting love surround us – we will all come home to a different world, whether we knew it was coming or not.

The rituals of death are the first steps to healing. It doesn't seem so while still in the misty veil of shock, interrupted by intermittent flashes of intense pain. But the time-honored ceremonies of your culture, honoring your loved one, hearing the stories, feeling the hugs of those who surround you with safety are essential. Offerings of food, people who love you standing by your side and holding you up, the visitation, the stories and memories, the funeral, the celebration of life, the conversations and tentative laughter at the dinner after. These are the first fleeting signs of the promise that life will go on – changed forever, but it will go on.

I researched funeral rituals of several different religions, nations, and belief systems. While there are many variations, the universal threads were the people gathering around the griever, and the preparation of food.

Following a recent tragedy, Sam Sifton, in the *New York Times* food section, wrote about grief and cooking. "Food plays a central role in our reaction to tragedy, to death, and grieving. It's why casseroles appear on doorsteps and countertops of those experiencing it, why we feel the urge to roast chicken or assemble lasagnas when the news is grim. Food is comfort of a sort, and fuel as well, for anger and sorrow alike. We cook to provide for those we love and for ourselves. In the activity itself, we strive to find relief, strength, resolve." [24]

We're carried. We're lifted. We're held.

But what happens when the rites of death are over, the rituals complete? What happens when your entire life feels composed of "this time last week" or "this time last month" as you confront this drastic change? The constant presence of others begins to wane. Their life goes on too – the life they put on hold to be there for you. They still call and check in, but over time, it will be up to you to let others know what you need.

You still have so much grief to get through. The protective misty veil slowly starts to lift, and the future lies before you, clearer, starker. As life's routines go on for others, another stage of your grief is just beginning.

Danielle Salmon Deschenes, a newly widowed mother of three boys, shares the challenges of life after her husband's unexpected death on her Instagram, @Danofish. "I grieve for the years you will miss, the days you are missing. I grieve that you won't get to see your children grow up. I grieve our plans that will never happen…I grieve for your children who don't have a father. I grieve for myself, as I've lost my best friend and most important person. I grieve the easy peaceful confidence that came from having a trusted partner and confidant in life. I grieve the end of a beautiful romance. I grieve the simpler easier life I used to have. I grieve the person I used to be, she doesn't exist anymore."[25]

At first, when someone we love dies, it leaves us empty of anything but sorrow. As we take the first uncertain steps toward healing that emptiness eventually holds space for memories, sweet and precious. They'll last a lifetime, bringing smiles to our lips, and meaning to our existence.

With notebook in hand, take a few minutes to reflect on your most difficult loss. What do you remember of those early days? Who do you remember? What did your first steps toward healing look like?

There are those of you reading this who didn't have support. You didn't have friends and family gathered around you. No one lifted you up and carried you through. You were alone due to age, geography, or circumstance. You read the previous paragraphs and felt worse because you missed having others to hold you. We'll address this in more detail when we discuss those who died during the pandemic, when all the rituals and foregathering were so cruelly disrupted. But please trust that there will be answers for you here. You might feel forgotten, but you are not.

In later chapters we'll develop a toolbox. It'll assist you in getting through each phase of your journey with universally helpful tasks, exercises, and information.

PART III: WHAT WE GRIEVE

Many other events lead to sorrow. It's important to hold space for each. In the following chapters you'll find my own and others' grief experiences and stories. Not all grief comes from death. There are other life changes that create sorrow. You might not have experienced loss but, by reading on, it'll help you understand what others are experiencing. You'll be supportive of those dear to you in their time of need. You may have experienced a loss that I don't include. If so, I'd like to hear your story.

Your grief story

With the journal entries, you've begun notes for your grief story. Now, we'll take the first steps in organizing it. We begin by creating a timeline. This is done, simply, with a horizontal line across a sheet, or sheets, of paper and marking your history with vertical notations along that line. Regular copy paper is all you need, making your line parallel to the longest edge. If you need more than one sheet, tape them together and continue your line. I recommend pencil for ease of editing. Either begin chronologically or start with your most significant losses and work from there. These will come to mind quickly. As you focus, other events and life changes will begin to surface. If it comes to mind, put it down.

Be prepared for feelings to rise up as you do this exercise. If you've experienced multiple losses, you may want to do this work in different sittings. This allows you a chance to spend time with those feelings, to honor them. Along with your timeline pages, keep your journal nearby. Writing these memories down and the feelings they bring will be another step in penning your grief story.

Your timeline and grief story are living documents. You'll likely add to them as additional memories occur to you. Keep them in a special drawer to be pulled out as needed. As your timeline leads to stories, they will be emotional and deeply personal. You'll feel vulnerable, yet strong, as you claim the courage to remember.

The timeline, and the notes you'll make throughout the chapters, might be the beginning of your story in detail, or it may remain the whole story. That's up to you. For myself and clients, I've found that it's helpful to take what you've written a step further by organizing and writing your narrative in more depth. As an example, I include my earliest conscious grief encounters. When I first started my own timeline, these came later, emerging from the trail of memories connected to my most significant life losses. Our grief lives in us. Every loss connects to what we've lost before. Documenting these life events is my grief story - which I share with you now.

My grief stories

My story begins when I'm nearly four years old with the death of the much-loved Nanny Ide, my great grandma. She lived a long life, but at three I had no concept of age. All I knew was she loved to play "going to the movies," "dress up," and "church Christmas program."

In those days, most visitations and viewings were held in the home. I have vague memories of being held in my father's arms looking down on her in the casket. I was asked if I wanted to touch her. I did not. I wanted to remember her as my laughing, waddly, open-armed Nanny who always had time to play whatever game I fancied. I wanted to remember how it felt to sit on her plentiful lap, my head resting on a pillowy bosom with her lavender-scented hanky stashed between the buttons of her housedress. She always stayed a part of me, and I shared her with my family. She made quilts. When I became an adult, I received a patchwork quilt she made and an unfinished quilt top. When my daughter went to college, I recut the top into a quilt for her dorm bed. I felt like I was passing on a part of my nanny to my daughter – four generations and counting.

What's your first memory of death or grief?

Another memory was the loss of small white handkerchief with embroidered blue cornflowers and scalloped edging. It was a gift from my Grandma Fern on my first day of school. It made me feel safe as I ventured away from the security of home. I was lost without it for a time and felt shame and sorrow that I hadn't taken care of it.

In second grade, there was the sadness of my best friend moving to California. Today, that would mean FaceTime calls and Zoom parties, but then it was the end of the world. I was too big to be rocked by my mama on most eight-year-old days, but the day of that news she held me in our brown Naugahyde rocking chair, gliding back and forth as I cried.

What about your first awareness that children die? How old were you when a tiny bubble of realization rose to the surface of your innocence – "I could die." "Maybe I will die." What kind of impact did it have? For me, two scenes come to mind immediately.

December 1, 1958. The day of Our Lady of the Angels school fire in Chicago. I didn't know anyone who died that day. But I grieved. Ninety-two children died, many eight-years-old like me, along with three nuns. Kids my age weren't supposed to die. I read devastating stories in the Chicago Tribune. I cut out pictures of the survivors. I cried for the families and the children who wouldn't go on. It was one of those national events that created turmoil beyond the boundaries of those directly affected. From then on, I occasionally pondered the possibility that I too could die.

At twelve, I lost a friend. She was three years older than me, but it was a small town and our lives intertwined through church and family activities. Also, she was an only child like me – a sort of club. She had an open friendly face and perfect brown bouffant hair. She was kind to everyone and played flute in the marching band. Her boyfriend from a neighboring town had his driver's license and seemed very grown up. They went to a movie one night and got hit head-on on their way home. Her boyfriend died instantly. My friend lived one more day. It was passed down through town lore that before she died, she told her mom that she heard angels singing. Everyone came to her funeral. Everyone cried. There was no doubt that she was loved and precious. Her mother never had the same smile again. Her spirit had gone with her baby girl. I thought of what my death would likely do to my mother. I just couldn't die.

It seemed that for a few years all I saw were mothers with empty hearts and eyes with perpetual tears. In the years after my high school graduation two classmates died in auto accidents. Another sweet girl, who married her high school sweetheart, died of a brain tumor leaving two small babies. Another family friend and his wife, parents of three toddlers, died in an auto accident when an elderly man crossed the center line. These were years of much sorrow for a small town of twelve hundred where every kid was everyone's kid. More awareness that I couldn't die.

Loss of a loved one, loss of a treasured keepsake, the departure of a friend, the first realization that children die too. You have your own. As you begin to focus, they'll emerge.

Daddy

My first major loss is the death of my dad. I was twenty-four. He was forty-four. His death and the death of my son were the first two entrants to my grief timeline. Though both were a long time ago, I remember them as if it happened yesterday. Think about your first major loss. Pay attention to your feelings. Does any of my story leave you angry or bring tears to your eyes? Any unexpected feelings?

To this day, I get angry at my dad on his brother's birthday. It happens every year. This year when my uncle turned ninety, Dad should've been ninety-one. But he's not. My uncle is still moving lawns and cleaning a few offices in my hometown. He still drives. He's still teasing his wife, and kids, and grands, and great grands. He got to enjoy his ninetieth birthday bash with his favorite cake and ice cream, and all his favorite people. He still shoots the breeze at the local coffee shop every morning at the table reserved for the old guys. Dad should be there too. But he's not.

Why? Because he likely drank too much and drove too fast. He died on a clear crisp October night on a corn lined country road, surrendering his life to an unsuspecting semi.

So, unreasonable, or not, I premise that, if not for that night of forty-four-year-old bad choices, he'd still be here. Yes. I'm aware fate could've taken him earlier, but he had the genes. He relinquished his right to try. And that makes me angry.

We've already acknowledged anger as a stage of grief, and that the stages aren't linear. We can go back and forth with bargaining, anger, depression, denial, acceptance. You never believe that these stages will continue through the rest of your life. But they do.

Anger. We all have reasons. What's yours? Who are you angry at for dying, or leaving, or getting sick? Who should still be here?

Just prior to that fateful night, I'd returned to my hometown after living out of state for three-years. I was married but still very much a daddy's girl. It was good to be back. The only downside was that I came back to my counseling role in the family. My parents were struggling after twenty-five years of marriage, and I was trying to help. In the process, I learned secrets I didn't want to know, and I thought I knew everything.

Let me tell you about my dad. Everybody loved Jimmy – a good guy, an honest man, the kind you want on your side in a fight. He had a bit of the daredevil in him. But he could always charm you with his boyish grin. A farm boy, he'd made good in the small town we called home. Always thoughtful and helpful, he mowed lawns and plowed snow for anyone he guessed might need it. And he never said no, if asked for a favor. He liked a beer after work with his buddies and had a regular poker night. He went to church now and then, but he'd fight you if he had too much whiskey. It made him mean and sometimes stupid. Though a giant of a man, he was short in stature. Whiskey liked to taunt him – called him a "short little bastard." Sometimes those lies got to him. But everyone loved him anyway, especially Mom and me.

He was forty-four years old and had worked his way up to managing a local Redi-mix company. He had what seemed a strong marriage to his high-school sweetheart. They'd recently celebrated their twenty-fifth wedding anniversary, figuring they'd make it through the present rough spot, as they always had before. Having raised me, only daughter, only child, they were now able to afford more trips and social activity that didn't revolve around their somewhat spoiled daughter.

Yes. Everybody loved Jimmy. On the night he died, it was his buddies on the fire department where he had once been chief, who used the jaws of life to get him out of his crushed car. News soon spread. Jimmy had been hit by a semi, dying instantly. My grandpa was the one who called, not knowing for sure how bad it was yet, or maybe he did and couldn't bear to tell me. He just said to come right away.

I quickly threw on my red and black wool poncho and raced to the car. It's funny what you remember. This poncho held a memory of riding in the back of a red '53 pick-up to see Easy Rider at my college town theater. The rage I felt after that movie became a thread in the fabric. I felt it every time I put it on. Now that event was eclipsed by it being the warmth around my shivers on the way to find out my dad was dead.

I spent the trip home in a one-sided conversation with my husband, hoping and praying that the injuries weren't severe, but would give him and mom the chance to step back from life and rebuild their marriage.

We went to my folks' house first. In the days prior to cell phones, we were still in the dark. As we drove up the driveway, I saw people just standing in the night, wandering aimlessly in the yard - people I knew. Dad's coworkers, morning coffee friends, moms and widows he had helped, church friends and bar buddies. They'd all heard the rumor, and just came to wait. Waited for the miracle of good news – that it had all been a mistake. They'd heard the likely worst from fireman husbands and mutual friends.

We drove on to the hospital where the yard wanderers said he'd been taken. As we pulled up, a longtime friend of my parents, a nurse I'd known since I was tiny, whose kids I'd babysat, who took me to my first musical in Chicago, stood at the ER door. She made eye contact. She barely shook her head. No miracle was coming.

I found Mom in a corner seat embraced by friends huddled around her. We crumbled together, and I let her cry and talk. He had come home late from his after-work beers at the tavern. They'd argued. She'd gone to bed when he left the house. She vaguely remembered hearing sirens in her sleep. Then she got the call. He died instantly they told us. He was still gone. A source of light and power and strength to so many, now just gone. Her husband. My daddy. Their friend.

My family doctor, since childhood, took me back to see him. Dad was curled up on his side on a gurney, his clothes, and shoes still on. He looked like he was sleeping, except for the side of his head that wasn't visible - except for the blood-soaked towel it rested on.

Then we moved in a haze, guided out of the hospital and home, walking through the friends still waiting with outstretched hands and soft words. Somehow, we slept. A fog of mental protection buffered the brain until there was some early grasping of reality. I found it came in fleeting moments of the veil fluttering open, as in a breeze, then wafting closed again.

The first of these moments came early the next morning. The phone rang. I answered. It was a friend of Dad's from out of town. He asked me if everything was ok, that he had heard something on the news. That was my first collapse, the first break in the fog telling me this was real. He was the first person I told that my daddy was dead. I felt as if the wind was knocked out of me, and I could no longer stand. But I did. Mercifully, the fog returned, and we moved through the rituals and necessities.

The food started coming in. The people came to help. The funeral director guided us through the steps we needed to take – the same funeral director, my friend's dad, who had taken us to see *Bye Bye Birdie* for his daughter's twelfth birthday in the hearse – the hearse that would carry my father's casket.

The people who brought kindness to the house stayed. It seemed there was always someone setting the table, someone standing at the oven, another with hands in a sink of sudsy water while other hands dried. Someone took to answering the constantly ringing phone. The footstool in front of my mom's chair was always occupied by someone with tissues who held her hand. My memory sense of those first days is that there were just always people surrounding our tiny cocoon of family grief. There was a spiritual lifting us up, carrying us, swaddling us in love.

My two grandmothers sat on the floor one of these early evenings, their backs against the wall and feet stretched out in front of them. They shared a rare beer. They got the giggles about something and laughed until, finally, they cried and cried. Hands helped them up and they hugged. Others wiped my dad's mother's first public tears, honoring the first break in her foggy shock.

The next flutter of the veil came when we had a family viewing before the visitation. I looked at my dad in the casket and saw the damage the accident had done. No matter how gifted our mortician, there was no covering the trauma the ER viewing had protected me from. I had a visceral moment of what felt like a scream then a physical effort to shut the casket. A kind person took care of me as the decision was made for a closed casket. A rush call went out to the local photographer who had recently taken Mom and Dad's anniversary pictures. He created a lovely photo of dad alone – so handsome with his sparkling brown eyes that always seemed to be harboring mischief.

It's strange. As much fog that sat over my heart, I remember every person who came through the two nights of visitation, and those who came up to us after the funeral. I remembered what everybody said about my daddy. It was the largest visitation the funeral home had ever had. Everybody loved Jimmy. I'd never thought much about the impact of rituals on a family before. After this, I never missed a visitation or funeral of anyone I knew or had a family member I knew. Those people who loved my father, walking by me, hugging me, crying with me, telling me a story – I never could've imagined the value of that without having experienced it.

One thing I noticed in myself as I faltered through the first days is "my dad" became "daddy" once again. And "died" became "killed." I hadn't called him daddy for years, but now I heard this come off my tongue and it somehow comforted me. I also noted the change from, he died in an auto accident to he was killed in an auto accident. It felt more active or something. That he had died somehow felt diminishing of his light, passively giving up. If he was killed, in my grief saturated mind, he put up a fight. It took effort to get him to leave us.

He was buried in a family plot in a country cemetery on a blue skied autumn day – on a hill under a tree where the soft breezes of summer and the harsh winds of winter came home. He was buried on his mother's birthday – in the veil, I don't know that any of us noticed until after that we had burned every future birthday with the image of her precious son being lowered into the ground.

I learned so much as I experienced this death. He was my first primary relative to die. There's so much you don't know until you've been through it.

I had no idea how much grieving there still is to do after the funeral and thank you notes. There are many ripple effects from a tragic death. My mother experienced a complicated grief. We'll look in more depth at this subject in a later chapter, but for this story I'll just say that circumstances left me in a situation of not only processing my own sorrow, but also trying to protect her – a role I knew well.

I spent time with Mom before I had to return to work in a nearby town. While the number of people in the house declined, she had faithful friends who still attended to her needs. Widowhood crystallized in tiny moments of discovery. There was the first time she put on a dress with a back zipper and realized she couldn't zip it. Dad had always done that for her. The same occurred with a necklace she had trouble with. Dad always did that tricky clasp. There was the buildup of dust on the plate rail. Dad took care of that. When the first snow fell, she shoveled the driveway for the first time in her life, her tears turning to ice on her cheeks. Slowly she put away his rings, his keys, his ties, his aftershave, his toothbrush. It took a long time to open his closet. It remained untouched for months.

After another few days, I passed the torch to my grandparents who lived a few blocks away. Their next weeks were consumed by taking care of Mom. We all got together every weekend.

Fortunately, Mom was the one who handled the finances, so she wasn't left in the dark. She also knew that Dad's company had kept a substantial keyman insurance policy in his name. There were, thankfully, not going to be any money concerns.

Leaving the cocoon of my family circle, opened a new level of sorrow as I began my life after. It felt alien to be away from people who knew my dad. I felt like I had traveled to an undiscovered planet. If they didn't know Jimmy, how could my friends grasp my pain? How could our neighbors and coworkers understand? But the caring was there. An hour after our return home, a bouquet of flowers was delivered from our next-door neighbors along with a casserole.

I found our home to be just the same as that night two weeks before. I picked up my pajamas off the floor and made the unmade bed. I stared at the phone in the bedroom where I had taken the call from my grandpa. I stood idly in front of the dining room hutch and was reminded of the Sunday before Dad was killed. He and Mom came for dinner. We just had macaroni and cheese, but for some reason I'd used my four place settings of good China now back in their place on the shelf. The leftovers were still in the fridge. At one point that Sunday, while watching a football game, Dad started to clip his fingernails. Mom told him to stop. Grandma Ide had been a superstitious sort and cutting your nails on Sunday was bad luck – forbidden. Something bad would happen if you broke the rule. He shhh'd her and finished. Three days later he was dead.

Am I superstitious? Not really. No worries about Friday the thirteenth or black cats. But the rule of no nail cutting on Sunday is strictly enforced.

The first thing I did when I returned to work a few days later was put a thank you note on the bulletin board by the time clock, which I reread every morning for a month until I took it down. The practice where I worked as a medical secretary had sent a beautiful plant (that I managed to keep alive for ten years) to the funeral home. My first days were filled with hugs in halls and caring coworkers popping into my office to see how I was doing. My desk was soon filled with notes, flowers, plants. Those who had had a parent die shared their grief stories. The planet wasn't so alien after all.

We attended an inquest into Dad's death a couple weeks later. It was like an out of body experience – hovering over the proceedings, watching the police and the firemen, his rescuers and friends, reading accident reports and drawing tire paths and lines on a chalk board – the jury declared his was an accidental death. I spent the night at my mother's. I suffered chills and chattering teeth for hours – a tough return to my body. The inquest was the official "closure." But the story continued long after.

When you get the chance to say good-bye

There were many additions to my grief timeline tucked in between my dad's death and the death of my son, and after. Those two were placed on that parallel line first because of the shock and tragedy that surrounded their loss. I said goodbye to other loved ones over the years. They were placed on my timeline next.

One gains a certain perspective once one hits seventy. I see all the lives I've lived, and how the people I've met along the way helped me to change and grow, to shape me and hone me. Looking back also gives me a view of the grief I've experienced – how the losses softened my heart and shifted my soul. I see what I learned, what I lost, and what I keep.

Madison Clark wrote in a *Daily Om* essay, "Opening ourselves up in this way gets to the core of our being, past all our defenses and prejudices. When life seems to crack the outer shell of our world, we are both raw and fresh at the same time."[26]

I was married with two small boys, and my first psychotherapy practice, when I began to lose my grandparents. I was close to all of them, but we lived across the street from my mom's folks during my early years. There was history between my mom and her mother from childhood, and they wanted to make up for what they missed. Both were committed to spending as much time together as they could. This resulted in our little family spending more time with Grandma Fern and Grandpa Joe, both by my mom's desire and the logistics of location. Just to clarify: Grandpa Joe was my step-grandfather, but the only one I'd ever known in that true role. (You'll hear of my biological grandpa later – in the Complicated Grief chapter.) We went to Sunday dinner every week at my dad's folks. They were dear to me, but my maternal grandparents were more like second parents. I don't recall ever having a hired babysitter. I always stayed with Grandma and Grandpa and rare overnights at my other grandparents' farm five miles out of town. Being awakened by crowing roosters – those were special events. It wasn't till later, as an adult, that I realized what a profound impact my connection to Grandma Fern had on my life.

The first grandparent I lost wasn't to death. It was to Alzheimer's. It had a different name back then – hardening of the arteries, I think. My spunky, always busy, Grandma Jean began to lose her train of thought playing cards and get confused while driving. Within months, she nearly burned the house down by leaving a stove on. When our boys came along, she could still love on them, but didn't remember after. By the time she was placed in a nursing home she didn't know any of us. Her body lived until 1992, but we said good-bye to her long before.

Grandpa Jim, my dad's dad, died in 1989 of heart failure. They called him Big Jim back in the day, and Dad, Little Jim. He was second generation German, hard-working, stubborn, and quiet. He was one man my dad would listen to if he needed a little talking to. I doubt if Dad ever talked to Big Jim about what was happening near the end of his life. He would've been too ashamed.

My grandma Fern died in 1990. She had a rare form of lymphoma that, after ten years, spread to her brain and lungs. She was tough. No one could stop her if she put her mind to something. My easy-going Grandpa Joe, when met with her indominable force, would just shake his head, and say, "Fern. Fern. Fern." She'd give him a kiss on the cheek and off she'd go. He'd gaze after her adoringly. In her last weeks she was placed on hospice in their home. Grandpa exchanged notes and Christmas cards with her hospice nurse, Jenny, until he died years later.

Both had enough time to say good-bye but, thankfully, not too much time to suffer. I got to whisper to my Grandpa Jim how much I loved him and that I knew I was always his favorite. I reminded him of those times he'd slip me twenty dollars for the boots I wanted or would talk my folks into letting me do something I wanted to do. I said thank you. I got a squeeze of my hand and a bit of a smile.

I was with Grandma the day before she died. She could no longer speak and was bed ridden. I read to her, reminisced to her. I lay on the bed beside her and told her all I wanted to say before she left me. She died in her own bed surrounded by Grandpa and Mom and nurse Jenny. Over the years, I probably wrote more about her than anyone else. As an adult, I encountered her handprint on my heart, her whispers in my soul. Years later, I held my Grandpa Joe's hand as he transitioned peacefully. He had a slight smile. I knew he was reuniting with his beloved Fern at last.

I grieved for these dear ones who had meant so much. I was comforted though, in the fact that they'd lived long productive lives. They'd given much to their work, communities, and especially those they loved. Though I might not have been ready, I knew they were prepared to say good-bye.

In these instances, death really did seem like closing the circle of life. That while their time on this earth was impermanent, it had been enough. That made it easier for me to let go of them. I had time to understand the gifts each had left me and take them to my heart.

I carried that feeling with me – until that peace was abruptly shattered on an early spring morning in March. Once again, I felt the earth tremble with the shock of loss.

Matthew

This is my story of the stillbirth of our son, his short life in my womb, and the months and years after. If you're a hurting heart with this painful loss, I hope you'll also sit down and write your story. It will leave you spent. It will break your heart. But Leonard Cohen tells us that light comes in through our brokenness. And a little more healing happens.[27]

After this, we'll spend time looking at the many faces of reproductive grief that also includes miscarriage, infertility, and abortion grief.

You'll find a poem I wrote for Matthew and excerpts of essays in Appendix A. These summarize what the loss felt like when they were written.

It seemed only fitting that two months after my grandmother Fern's death I became pregnant with our third son. Gram always enjoyed our boys. Even when stiff with pain, she managed to get down on the floor and play with them. She would've been delighted with one more great grandbaby.

The plan was for this to be our last. I'd be forty and we were so lucky to have our beautiful family. I loved being pregnant, the primal feeling of my body doing what it was created to do. We laughed that it was a good thing we started late, or we would've had ten kids.

So, we took a third pregnancy in stride – old hands at it by now. But I also cherished it, knowing it would be the last. We were living in a small house that was already stretched beyond its limit, so we bought a larger home. We picked the room for the nursery and went about fitting it out. Life progressed smoothly as we prepared for baby Matthew Joseph. Each of our boys had a family member's middle name. His was from my Grandpa Joe. He was due in April. A redbud tree grew outside of the nursery window. I'd envision standing there holding him and pointing out its beauty to his newborn eyes that spring. At Christmas we hung a new stocking. On Christmas morning, "Santa" had filled everyone's stockings, including a small plush duck peeking out of Matthew's.

When I was thirty weeks pregnant, my blood pressure started to be borderline high. Nothing to be alarmed about, but I needed to rest more and get off my feet. I'd stop at the doctor's office between appointments for a blood pressure check and to hear Matthew's heartbeat. One Monday I stopped by, chatted with the nurses, and waited for an exam room. Once there, my blood pressure checked out okay, but they couldn't find a heartbeat. Nobody seemed concerned, figuring he was just in some strange position, but "let's do a sonogram to take a look." As I write this, I can still close my eyes and see his quiet little spine and ribs – and hear the deafening silence of the still life screen. No movement. No heartbeat. No life. It was a slow-motion film, without sound until nurse Sharon said softly, "Oh Vicki. I'm afraid we have a problem."

Then, I'm sitting in my doc's office. I know all his plaques and diplomas and certifications by heart, having been his patient for thirteen years. I remember when he got the hole in one recorded on one plaque. He was so happy showing it off to my husband, he nearly forgot about his pregnant patient. There's the huge frame filled with pictures of newborns and his big grinning face leaning into the picture with Mom and Dad, photo Christmas cards of "his babies" as they grew. Like most women, I loved my obstetrician a little bit. This was where the happiest moments of my life happened.

I called my husband who worked thirty miles away and carpooled. I really don't remember my words. The next thing I remember is watching out the window as he drives up in a red Cadillac convertible that one of his coworkers loaned him for his agonizing drive. To this day, seeing a car like that tweaks my heart.

Somehow, we got through the talk with our doc, though his words seemed to come from a long echoing tunnel. We digested options and agreed to induce my labor the next day to lessen the risk of infection.

Somehow, we got home and held it together to tell our boys that their baby brother had died in Mommy's tummy. Their innocent questions broke my broken heart again. Calls were made to family and friends. Arrangements made. Help accepted.

My mother-in-law arrived to care for the boys while we went to the hospital the next day. I remember the crystal-clear blue sky that morning, smelling of spring, of new life.

I was admitted to a labor bed. A phlebotomist was there to draw my blood. I was in labor and delivery with a pregnant belly. Unaware of my situation, she smiled as we heard a newly delivered newborn cry. "You'll be hearing your own baby soon." I didn't have the heart or energy to tell her I wouldn't hear my baby cry.

The next hours I felt near death as prostaglandins, injected to induce labor, set about dropping my blood pressure and sprouting a fever of 103 degrees and a pulse of 140. Our young priest sat with my husband in the room. We found out later that a large group we'd never met from a dear friend's church sat in the waiting room and prayed for us throughout the day. If there was a time for God to carry us, it was this.

Late in the day, a Tuesday's child like his brothers, our beautiful Matthew Joseph was gently delivered and silently placed in my arms, in that crook of the elbow created for a baby's tiny head. My husband and I went through all the age-old motions of checking fingers and toes, touching his hair, kissing his cheek, but our tears fell wet on his face, as we grieved for his eyes that wouldn't open, for the lips that wouldn't utter a cry. Father Joe baptized him in my arms. The veil of early grief was merciful. We went into an autopilot of numbness.

When I woke up the next morning in the hospital, I found a gift bag from a friend and coworker with crayons and coloring books for the boys and a book for me, *A Crocus in the Snow*. It was inscribed "To Vicki and Matthew – whose song will sing in the hearts of those who loved him forever." That inscription so lovingly and thoughtfully gifted made it real. For that moment my heart was clear of any fog. My baby had died.

We were able to hold him two more times, spending time saying good-bye, telling him about his big brothers and how we had dreamed his place into our family that would forever remain. We chose not to bring the boys to the hospital, deciding they might be too young. I regret that now. As they got older, they both wished they could've seen him.

Friends and family surrounded us, held us, fed us, played with the kids, made calls, did laundry. They came to spend the day when my husband had to return to work. I remember one friend, telling me that after this kind of loss some would start screaming and never stop. There was a stormy day that was do dark, it seemed like nightfall. I wonder if that perception was real or just a gray day imprinted with my own darkness.

We had a funeral mass in my hometown. He was buried near my dad and grandparents in the cemetery on the hill under a still-bare maple tree. Matthew wore his blue going home sleeper with an airplane on the front and was tucked into a tiny white casket, cuddled in his baptism blanket. My husband had a primal need to carry his son's casket from the hearse to his burial spot. I know it felt like it was the only thing he could do for his boy. It's a helpless feeling when you're the one who takes care of and protects your family - to have nothing left to do but carry a casket. We grieved together for our son, but we also had to grieve in our own ways over the next weeks.

Matthew died just before Easter. My birthday and Mother's Day came soon after. The church had a memorial service for parishioners who died the past year. It was a week after Matthew's funeral. I still wore maternity clothes. We sat there as Father read his name – "Matthew Joseph Mitchell." It was the first time I heard it in such a context. You know, the whole name, like he was being announced to walk across the stage and get a diploma. But instead of yells and whistles from his cheering section, we all got up and silently lit his candle.

Caring folks told me this was a part of God's master plan. I thought to myself, well God should've had a Plan B that didn't include taking my son. People told me Matthew was with Jesus, and he was happy. I'd watch his brothers playing football in the backyard, decked out in their Chicago Bears uniforms from the past Christmas. And I'd say to my husband, "Heaven might be great, but I can't imagine a little boy who wouldn't rather be playing football with his brothers."

I went to a bookstore in search of books that might bring me comfort and maybe answers. I found the book. It was a skinny, paperback children's book called *The Fall of Freddy the Leaf*, by Leo Busgalia. It was the story of what Freddy discovered as he went through his life cycle of seasons, so familiar to my Midwestern heart. I sat cross-legged in the aisle as I read this remarkably simple book, and I cried. I gave away my copy long ago, but when I decided to start this work, it was the first book I bought for reference.[28]

My forty-first birthday was a dazed affair. The boys and their dad made me a cake and decorated the traditional "birthday chair." My well-meaning in-laws came and took me to lunch at a favorite local restaurant. They told the staff it was my birthday. Soon after lunch was finished, a little cake with a candle was placed in front of me. Suddenly, there was a dark cloud of sombreros shadowing over me as the staff sang "Happy birthday," accompanied by maracas and tambourines. Though a thoughtful and well-meaning act, the photo taken during the festivities reflects my near panic.

Days blurred together. I could tell I was moving forward in tiny steps. I no longer sat in his nursery rocking the giant teddy his uncle had sent for him. Shower time became a haven. I could shut the door, turn on the spray and my sobs were drowned out. Or so I thought. My husband told me later that he could hear every cry.

When the pressure of feelings became too much, I'd go for a ride and park in a secluded spot along Grandview Drive overlooking the Illinois River, the one Teddy Roosevelt deemed "the most beautiful drive." There I would scream and wail until there was nothing left.

My boys grieved by talking about their brother, playing imaginary games, drawing pictures. One morning I found my oldest climbing into the crib as they started a game. I lost it in a very non-motherly way, shouting at him to get out of Matthew's crib. In his practical five-year-old voice he said, "But Mom, Matthew isn't going to ever get to use it." Then I crumbled and cried, and my sweet five-year-old comforted me. While driving my youngest son to childcare, I noticed he was near tears. When asked how he was feeling, he said in his almost three-year-old voice, "I'm sad because my brother Matthew Jophes died."

Sometime in the following weeks, I got a call from the hospital that Matthew's nursery newborn pictures had arrived if I wanted them. In a perverse, pitiful way, this brought me momentary joy. He felt alive for a minute – just the normalcy of newborn pictures. They were the last thing I would ever receive from Matthew. There was nothing else left. There wouldn't be any stick figure mommy pictures, or dried leaves and rocks placed in my palm, or first tooth to come out, or sticky little boy kisses. I would never see his homework in his backpack, hold his soccer medal, dance the mother-son dance at his wedding. This was it.

One month later, I returned to work. I came back to my office on the day my maternity leave was supposed to begin. It was good to get back to a sense of normal, but I was unprepared for the growth I was about to experience as a therapist. Each of my clients had their own grief to process about my absence, their loss, my loss, and how it impacted them.

Another layer of vulnerability revealed itself in my heart. My total presence was imperative in helping them through the pain and confusion. I was the strong one, the one they thought carried all the answers. Some of my clients got upset when one of my plants needed water. How could they trust me to help them if I didn't water my plants? Now this! I was the one who helped them through suffering, not the other way around. There was anger, abandonment, fear. There was caring, empathy, tenderness. One client had guilt because she had a dream that my baby died. Another had a psychotic episode as she feared her thoughts about my baby had caused his death. Old boundaries that seemed so safe were being pushed and rearranged. As my grief mingled with theirs, we both grew. The therapist I was when I retired has a direct connection to what my clients and I experienced in those first weeks.

By Mother's Day, I was able to get through twenty-four hours without tears. My in-laws came for dinner, and my husband and I went to a special concert at the local cathedral. It was a day to treasure my boys. Every day that I didn't think I was going to make it, their smiles, cuddles, and silliness got me through.

On that chilly Mother's Day, we planted Matthew's apple tree in the backyard. We would watch it grow and blossom and bear fruit. We've long since moved from that house, but I check on it when I go by. It now towers over the neighbor's garage. I fear one day it'll be gone. I don't know what I'll do.

I kept a grief journal for about six months. It was put away in Matthew's special memory box. That yellow spiral notebook with an Easter cross sticker on the front wasn't re-opened until I started this project. I was having problems getting words on the page. Finally, I admitted that the unread journal held me back. I'd never write honestly about grief if I didn't face the grief held between the notebook covers. I went to my room, closed the door, and started reading the words I wrote nearly thirty years ago. I wept for the tear in our family's fabric. Then I took a few minutes to see my life now – the good that came from Matthew's sacrifice, the lovely daughter, now a wife and mother, who is my rainbow baby, my strong adult sons with families of their own, the strength of my marriage. Then I started to write.

Matthew's death is my greatest loss. But every loss pulls all the rest together. Each loss changes you.

I can remember the exact moment that I realized I was healing. It was in a most inconsequential way. I loved *Bon Appetit and Country Living* magazines. I'd savor my quiet time after everyone else was in bed to sit down with a cup of tea and read every page. I'd note recipes or decorating ideas. For a few months after Matthew died, I couldn't have told you if these treasures had arrived in the mail. But one night, as I came to bed, I noticed a *Country Living* sitting on the bedside table. I picked it up. I leafed through it - with interest. It was then that I knew I was healing. I picked up a beautiful cross stitch project that I'd worked on throughout my pregnancy. I thought maybe I was ready to finish it but couldn't. Matthew was in every thread. The piece was titled "Rose of Sharon." I may not have been able to finish the cross stitch, but every yard I've planted since has that beautiful flowering shrub.

Healing began, but there were still moments that brought me, once more to my knees.

On a memorable trip to Toys R Us, I was walking down an aisle and a mom carrying a tiny pink bundle of baby came toward me. I had an immediate flight or fight response and literally ran from the store. I ended up in my car, sitting there until I could collect myself. It wasn't even a baby boy.

We stopped by a friend's house one morning to drop off something. We were just in the foyer talking to the husband, barely inside the door. His wife started down the stairs with their four-month-old. I saw the edge of a blanket and tiny bare toes. The next thing I remember I was in the car trembling. These primal responses were frightening.

The boys took swim lessons at a local pool that summer. I was able to relax and watch them relishing in their new skills, and even enjoyed the sunshine. That is, until a mother with children in the class entered poolside carrying a chubby-thighed fivish-month-old baby boy – so healthy and pink and wiggly and wild. I made it through the lessons by moving, nonchalantly, to the other side of the pool, but I was transfixed. This time, I couldn't take my eyes off the baby. I wanted him to be mine. When we got home, the boys played with Daddy. I went to take a shower for my cry.

The boys grew. My oldest started kindergarten in the fall. The following March, the monthly all-school Mass was said for Matthew. Father, who generally, just said the name of the person, told the children that Matthew was a baby who'd died before he was born and that he was with Jesus. As I sat there with tears streaming, another mom came to sit by me. A mother of six children, she told me her daughter had died when she was seven months pregnant. We cried together.

I liken my recovery to a city that's been bombed. The visual image came to me of a European city bombed during WWII, and how the city healed, and flowers bloomed again, and parks reappeared. But a crater remained among the flowers and the trees and the laughter and the peace. Life went on. The city thrived. But the bomb crater was a memorial of the suffering, of that horrible time in history when they lived in fear and sorrow, and they didn't know if they'd survive. That's how I see my heart – with an unfillable hole surrounded by flowers, summer breezes, and laughter. It's teeming with life. But the crater remains.

My career progressed. My husband, who made the never-ending drive from his work to the doctor's office that horrible day, chose to leave that job he loved and took a position at a local company. He didn't want to be that far away again. We were active in church, kids' schools, and sports. A little over a year later, we got pregnant again. It was hard to feel excited or hopeful, though we wanted another child very much. When I was eight weeks pregnant, blood appeared in my underwear in a bathroom stall one Sunday morning. By the next day, I'd had a D&C and the baby was gone – the baby that was only a heartbeat on a sonogram and a pink plus on a stick and in my dreams – the baby I was afraid to get excited about. I grieved this child too, but it almost felt pre-ordained that I would miscarry. After this, we decided our childbearing years were over. We were blessed with two beautiful boys who brought us constant joy. It was time to let go the dream of more.

But I continued to feel unfinished. There was a gaping hole. Every kid story was destined to end with "It should've been Matthew's." Last child's first Christmas, last child to stop nursing, last child to be potty trained, last child's first day of school. I was forty-three and the restlessness in my soul, the incompleteness of my biology, told me I wasn't done having children.

I only recently heard the term, rainbow baby, referring to the next child you have after a loss. That's what my daughter was and is – bringing sunlight and color back to my reproductive life cycle. She closed the circle. Now Matthew was in the middle of my story rather than shadowing the end. He was tucked between his big brothers and his baby sister. My daughter, now in her twenties with a baby girl of her own, thought for years that she was an accident. When I heard this, I laughed. There aren't many women in their forties who take their temperature for months to hit that chance of conception.

All my children are precious and valuable. I couldn't have survived the first weeks and months after Matthew died without my boys who saved me every day with their laughter, love, and honesty. My lovely daughter cured the nagging ache of my arms, the emptiness of my womb. She completed my pregnancy story, the circle of my womanhood, and showed me how to be a mother to a daughter, and all the joy that brings.

Yet the chasm that would be Matthew in the family remains permanent. He meant something to all of us, not just me, his mom. He will live forever in our hearts. His is one of the roses in the memorial vases at weddings. He is there in the book read on Christmas eve, on the tree, and the fourteenth stocking hung on the mantel. He is at the table when someone decorates an Easter egg for him. His legacy lives on.

Death of a child

Joan Didion wrote in *Blue Nights*, a memoir of the death of her daughter, "What greater grief can there be for mortals than to see their child dead?"[29] There is none.

My friends said many things in their efforts to comfort me, trying to make sense of a senseless loss. One said that I had now survived the worst thing that could ever happen to a parent, but deep down I feared there could still be worse. I had other children. I knew my heart would never be safe again, that another loss such as this would take my last breath.

My boys lived through a period of ultra-conservative parenting as I shielded them away from anything I deemed unsafe. In her novel, *Dinner at the Homesick Restaurant,* Anne Tyler's mom character, Pearl, was shocked and frightened by how much she loved her first child. Her solution was to have more children, thinking that the more she had, this overwhelming love would just spread out among them, diluting it somehow. After three, she discovered she was now even more vulnerable as she loved each one of them beyond measure. "What she had now was not one loss to fear but three."[30]

Nothing is guaranteed. Once you accept the responsibility and the sweetness of parenting, you accept the risk of bone crushing loss. When you hold your newborn, your own or adopted, you're initiated into a love so deep and pure, you never could've imagined it. You're terrified something will happen to her. But the truth is that when they crawl, walk, swing you'll somehow be ready. When they go to school, sleepovers, camps, and get behind the wheel, you'll somehow be prepared. Your heart goes with them. Also, a little fear. But not all of it. We couldn't survive the constant stress of the panic that can come when we hear a cry from a next room, or see a flipped over sled, or stare at a ticking clock ten minutes past curfew. It's those times that fear jumps out like a genie from a lamp and surrounds us with a paralyzing terror. Then you walk in the room and find a ball has rolled under the couch, or the fall from the sled harmless, or you see the headlights in the driveway. Then the fear retreats – kept at bay by the reality that we must let our children grow up.

But we always know, as much as we plan for their safety, sometimes the worst can happen. The medical miracle doesn't materialize. The bookcase topples. The car can't stop on the ice. The phone rings and the end of our world is here.

Everything about the stages of grief, complicated grief, and tools for healing apply to the death of your child. The pain, the anger, the "if onlys" are magnified. The need for support is overwhelming. The healing takes longer and looks different. You'll carry the sorrow with you as you navigate the path to life ever after.

Yes. There will be a life "after." You'll feel joy again. But your journey is the most difficult anyone should ever be called to travel. You'll find your way, but I'm not so presumptuous as to tell you I have the answers. There will be reasons to keep going. You'll find your "why." For me, it was my two little boys. I was broken. Weak. Helpless. But I gained a bit more strength each day as they brought me dandelions, and dirt, and butterflies and crickets. They also brought me smiles and a heart of gratitude.

You'll find a way to honor the life of your child. You may become a fighter for legislation to prevent another parent from going through what you have. You'll take your horror and bring about change or attention to a need.

If you, or a loved one, is going through this loss, please seek help. This isn't a journey to embark on alone. You may think that you and your partner can survive this by leaning on each other, but you must give each other time to also grieve separately. Many couples divorce following a child's death. The burden of personal grief, and each other's sorrow can be insurmountable. As much as you love each other, there will likely be feelings that arise for each of you, warranted or not, like shame, guilt, anger, blame as your brain tries to find a place to put this pain. These feelings need to be processed and dealt with. Forgiveness is a step toward healing. A professional can help with this.

Be prepared for ambivalence toward your friends with children. Their need to support you will be obvious, but you might feel anger at the fact that they still have their children. And you know that, no matter how present they are, they go home in the evening and get to hug their kids and thank heaven that your loss is not theirs.

Throughout these pages there are words written especially for you, directed to your heart, your pain, your movement forward. May they bring you comfort and a lifeline for the next step.

Reproductive Loss

I hope that by sharing my experience I can assure you, once more, that even the darkest times can be brought into the light. Because of my own loss, my office became a haven for hundreds. I could give parents the professional guidance they needed, but also offer the sympathy of a survivor. That was important at a time when they weren't sure they could make it through what they felt. And in helping them I could bring good from my pain.

After essays I wrote about reproductive loss (Appendix A) were printed, I started receiving letters and emails from other mothers, fellow grievers, who had experienced miscarriages and stillbirths, as well as women who suffered from infertility or trauma from abortion. It was this outpouring that led to my professional focus on reproductive grief.

There is so much silent mourning among parents who lose a child not yet born. Their sorrow deserves a voice. I sensed that from the letters and those I later counseled. But before that, I saw it in all the tear glistened eyes of women who shared with me after Matthew died, most of whom I had no idea had experienced such loss.

I was a member of a club that no one wants to join. The dues are high and it's a lifetime membership. It's a sort of secret society, as you aren't always aware of who belongs until you pass through the rites of initiation. Then, seemingly within minutes, the women who have known such sorrow surround you and begin a chorus that sustains.

One of my labor nurses during Matthew's birth had been my maternal-child nursing instructor. Though I'd known her since nursing school, I only then learned she lost a baby girl when she was six months pregnant. She didn't see the baby. No one told her how sorry they were. No one said she should take time to grieve. It wasn't meant to be they said. You can try again they said. She went home, having no idea why she felt so sad and empty for months after.

The support group continued to gather with cards, phone calls and visits from acquaintances and friends who shared similar experiences. It seemed everywhere I went, there was someone else God sent to keep me going.

A woman who worked in my boys' preschool office shared with me that her baby was diagnosed with leukemia at six-months old and died six months later. Her infant's loss was honored as a tragic death, but she shared that she felt pressure to move on, to try again, to "replace" her child.

A young lady at church reached out to share she had a stillbirth at eight months also. She named her baby boy after her father. Her fear was she would never have another son.

A new friend who we met a few months before I became pregnant with Matthew shared her story. Seven years earlier, she was nine months pregnant with her baby girl. She went to the hospital in early labor. Everything looked fine so she was sent home to rest. Once her labor became more active, she returned to the hospital only to find her baby girl had died in those few hours.

There were stories of loss, of multiple miscarriages, infertility. I was now a person who understood their pain, as I was steeped in my own, I think the most heart-rending moment was when I was at the grocery story with my younger son in the grocery cart seat. We were at the frozen food case as an elderly lady came from the opposite way. She stopped and looked at my red-headed three-year-old. She smiled a sweet smile and tears filled her eyes. She told me she had a baby boy who looked a lot like my son who had died at birth. She touched his hair. We hugged. And she walked on.

It was then that it hit me right there in the aisle of frozen vegetables – I'm never going to get over this! It was my first inkling that at a moment's notice a thread can be tugged, and the feelings can be called to the surface when we least expect it.

I was ignorant to the reality that these women didn't know what to do with that pain. I didn't know, until arriving in their shoes, that there was this huge hurt in them that presented an awkwardness in speaking to the uninitiated. I discovered this myself and it sensitized me to the limbo of death before "life."

When do you share? Certainly not in a conversation with a woman who is eight months pregnant. What do you say when asked how many children you have? What do you say when a group of women are sharing birth experiences?

It is, at times, viewed as a faux pas to talk of death and pain and the insurmountable anguish of a labor predestined for grief. It creates a break in the otherwise light conversation when you talk about having three children and one in heaven. No one knows quite what to do with it. Then if anyone is courageous enough to ask, there tends to be a little sigh of relief that it was "only" a stillbirth or miscarriage – not a real live child who died.

This isn't intentional sensitivity. It is just that you cannot truly know until you've been there.

But I believe understanding can come. If more of us take the risk to share our pain, then more will be aware that there is pain. If we don't, how will anyone know what it's like to feel the silence in your womb? How will anyone know this baby has a place in the family just as your other children do? Who will share the sorrow of hearing a baby's first cry in the labor room next door, knowing only silence will come from your room today? Who will talk of what it's like to return home to the nursery left empty?

And who will take the risk of sharing what Mother's Day was like six weeks after the loss of a child, so thankful for the gifts of joy and love from your other children, but empty arms aching for the baby you will never again hold?

As a professional in a helping field, it's important that I validate my hurt and that of others. Fortunately, there also comes joy as I acknowledge not only the suffering but also the healing. Life does go on and the heart finds freedom from the daily agony of remembrance. That agony, though sometimes still as fresh as the day it came, is also transposed with the memory of a life that was, the joy he brought to my heart and the change he inscribed on my soul.

Miscarriages, stillbirth, neonatal loss, and infertility

You may have other reasons for reproductive grief than a stillbirth or early miscarriage. Adult and teen women and men, couples, families came to me with many stories of sorrow.

There's no gauge to define if one loss is harder than another. The couple who experiences multiple miscarriages, or struggles with infertility, who bear stillbirths or neonatal loss, or are dealing with the emotional toll of abortion carry a common thread of pain.

It's important to hold space for even the earliest loss, where your only relationship with your baby is through a sonogram heartbeat and a dream. The bonding and the plans for this tiny being growing inside you begins at once. It's been said miscarriage is harder on the woman because her relationship starts immediately, while her partner tends to begin more serious bonding once the baby is born. I didn't find that to be the case. Each parent may have a different relationship with this babe, but the emotional toll on their hearts and their coupledom is carried mutually.

Stress strains marriages to breaking points with the fear, feelings of failure, and loss of multiple miscarriages. Every loss is mourned, even if others mouth all the well-meaning platitudes of those who've not experienced a pregnancy loss. Sex becomes regimented, anticipated with grim determination and dread rather than affection, intimacy, and pleasure. Talking about it becomes difficult. Guilt or blame over who has "the problem" becomes an issue. Anger and frustration invade a once happy home.

Every story you hear about a woman who has multiple children but little interest or ability to take care of them enrages you. That life should be so unfair, that an abusive parent, a neglectful mother, an addicted father should have children and you're left with empty arms, never feels okay.

If a couple chooses in vitro fertilization, new problems loom. The cost creates financial stress. The mood-altering chemicals and procedures add new variables to an already vulnerable relationship. If the IVF is unsuccessful, the loss is profound. If the IVF is successful, only to end in miscarriage, the burden can feel unbearable.

Counseling and support groups can be helpful in both the navigation of the process and dealing with the grief. If you make it to parenthood, whether a biological birth or adoption, all will seem worthwhile. If you're left with adapting to a life without children, it's a whole other journey to finding peace.

For my clients, the outcomes were as varied as the options. I saw happy high functioning couples destroyed. I saw failed IVFs where the twosome found a path to being a family without children. But I also saw success for a couple who went on to have two lovely daughters, a result of two separate IVF pregnancies. I saw their relationship heal, when at one point it seemed doomed. I saw IVFs where babies were born prematurely and died. I saw couples forced to make heartbreaking decisions about how many embryos to keep. I saw successful pregnancies after five miscarriages. I saw a full-term baby stillborn after a successful IVF ended with a ruptured uterus. This couple survived and went on to adopt two siblings at birth.

Even adoption is not without risk and cost, both financial and emotional. We tend to say "you can always adopt" as if it were a simple process. If you're fortunate enough to be able to financially afford it, there is a grueling process of paperwork, home visits, and decisions. If, after months of preparation and work, you're approved, it's only the beginning. Now you must make hard decisions about which pregnant women will see your portfolio. Then the waiting to be chosen begins. If you're not quickly selected by a birth mother the stress and tension of why not and what's wrong with us has a way of niggling into the coupledom. After a while, it all begins to feel like a sixth-grade playground waiting to be picked for the team, afraid you'll be last. Once selected, there's the fear the birth mom will change her mind. But, if patient, there is more often than not, a happy outcome with regrets and frustration left behind. Ask anyone. They'll tell you it's worth it.

I saw marriages weather all the storms. I saw marriages fail, some even after a successful birth. There are no easy answers. It's unique in that so much of your sorrow is that of a dream, a picture of how you always thought your life would unfold but instead being forced to take detours of loss and pain.

Many of the journeys I shared included neonatal loss or stillbirth. Whether it be a genetic issue, a developmental anomaly, prematurity, or an accident, it was a precious child who, by all rights, should be here but isn't. There's no easy way to recover from this. But, like any loss, we process the pain, we move toward healing, and we try to create some good.

Abortion grief

Abortion grief is often ignored. Our society would have us believe that it's an objective decision to abort – a choice of convenience or timing. But in most cases, it's gut-wrenching and painful.

My masters research project focused on the topic of women who have abortions and future risk of depression. It was a survey study so not the most reliable, but it did show a statistically significant correlation. I can tell you, without hesitation, that I treated many women for depression, and an abortion was in a significant number of their histories. But what seemed most telling was even the most open and verbal person tended to share the abortion last. A woman would tell me illegal, immoral, unsavory, abusive, and guilt-ridden events in their history, but the last thing they would confess was the abortion they had in their teens or college years. Some recounted the anguish of their decision. Others shared that, at the time, it didn't seem to be an emotionally charged issue. It was after they had their first child that it hit them. Or if they had infertility or miscarriage issues, they felt it was punishment.

It wasn't only women I saw for abortion grief. I spent time with men whose partner chose to terminate a pregnancy they had fathered, or later years guilt over coercing a sexual partner into an abortion.

Both men and women must make the journey of healing and recovery. This is often a silent, unsupported journey, never shared with anyone but their therapist. The tools and advice offered in the later chapters are also for you.

All reproductive grief has complicating factors that benefit from counseling and support groups. If you've experienced any reproductive loss, please take time to honor that loss, that tiny person, that dream, that hole in your heart. I understand this is a difficult request, but I'd like you to take out your journal and write a letter to your baby or babies not with you. Share what you imagined for her, how you felt if you got to hold him, how sorry you are. This is also a chance to face any shame or guilt you might carry by also writing a letter to yourself – a chance for self-forgiveness. While painful, you'll find this to be a cathartic act of connection and love.

Suicide

Every loss leaves questions. Some are answered. Most aren't. The questions become mountains of "if onlys" and "whys" if the loss is by suicide. They seem insurmountable. A loved and valued person chooses to exit this earth, and we're left with a lifetime of wondering.

I encountered the subject of suicide daily. At the hospital, all new admissions were asked directly if they were having thoughts of suicide. A history of thoughts, plans, intent, and attempts was explored, and if anyone close to them had attempted or completed a suicide. A person close to the patient was also interviewed and asked about recent changes in behavior – giving things away, saying good-byes, mood improving, tying up financial loose ends. It was a thorough and methodical process. Gathering this data saved lives. It made us aware of the potential for suicide and the patient was aware that we cared, were listening, and were going to make every attempt possible to keep him safe. We engendered hope that things would get better, given time and space, and a safe place.

There was no guarantee. A person could be on suicide precautions, checked every fifteen minutes, whereabouts monitored, and any potentially dangerous items removed. There could still be a completed suicide. You don't forget them – the ones you saved or the ones you lost. There was the teen-age boy with beautiful blue eyes and long blond hair who came to me to confess he ate pencil lead and was going to die. A check with poison control revealed that pencils are now made of graphite and non-lethal. He was placed on suicide precautions. He talked about his future, thankful for another chance. Yet two weeks later he hung himself in his room.

There was the gentleman who packed a gun in his hospital bag, and before the nurse could go through his things during admission shot himself. There was the elderly woman, widowed and alone, who said she found new reasons to live while she was hospitalized. She went home and cut her throat with a broken glass. There was a young man who hung himself from the inside of his room door, never having uttered a suicidal thought. There was the young woman, a poet and musician with much to live for, who denied any desire to die. Upon discharge she road tripped to Colorado in late fall. She hiked to a high elevation, removed her clothes, folded them neatly on a rock, laid down and went to sleep.

Too many are lost. Too many questions left unanswered. How do you tell your preteen son that a twelve-year-old boy on his junior football team killed himself with a shotgun? What do you say to his parents at the funeral? How do you comfort parents of a thirteen-year-old who impulsively took an overdose of his dad's heart medicine – unable to be saved – the last words they heard – "Please don't let me die. I don't want to die."

How do I express the emotional relief of a therapist when a widower tells her, after the fact, that in the first weeks we worked together, he had a tarp laid out in his basement, a gun loaded, and a note instructing his daughter to remain upstairs and call 911?

My mantra to all was – "It always gets better. It always gets better. It always gets better." Even when there were times I didn't see how it was going to get better, I knew it would. And, given the chance, it always did.

There are more stories, most of saved lives, but also of those we lost. When I began this work, I felt prepared for the sorrow and the fear. Brought up by my beloved, vulnerable parents, threats of suicide were a part of my life. Growing up, they were only threats. Mostly I overheard them during fights. But my mother would also tell me tearfully with a tight hug, that I was the only thing that kept her alive. A lot of therapy, years later, lifted that burden. It eased my guilt-ridden soul when she made a suicide attempt years later. You might wonder if my dad committed suicide. I wonder too. We knew he was drinking. We knew he was driving fast. We knew an inquest, with a jury of men who loved and respected him, found his death accidental. There was no note, no recent actions or words that might have set off alarms. My mother never let the thought that he might have done this intentionally enter her mind. But I knew he carried a heavy burden.

The experience of eight years nursing on a mental health unit and growing up caring for my parents did not prepare me for out-patient therapy. When I left the mental health unit to begin my career as a therapist, I was ready to begin this next phase. No more weekends or holidays except for when on call. The freedom to make my own schedule allowing me to be a perennial room mother and never miss an event. I had a lovely office that I got to decorate, and colleagues I respected. I couldn't ask for more.

But I found myself accosted with new anxieties about my depressed clients who had suicidal thoughts. Even though I did the same suicide screening questions as I did for in-patients, I tended to overdo safety contracts. I was prone to admit anyone who I felt the least bit anxious about to the hospital. It was then I began a long and fruitful relationship with a therapist who was my sounding board whenever I needed it throughout my career. Yes. Therapists need therapy too. Especially good therapists. And through my work, I discovered that I kept trying to save my parents, and that translated into my fears about my clients. When I worked through those fears and anxieties, I was a better therapist. I was able to be more present and tolerate the risk that accompanied letting a client work through their feelings. I discovered I had to trust them for them to learn to trust themselves. I became a guide and participant in their healing rather than their over-protective, hovering rescuer, the role I had played with my mother since early childhood.

I understood that there were some situations where a client could not find another way out of his pain. Suicide, to that person, was the only option. In those moments, whether it be emotional or physical pain, the right to choose death cannot be judged. These are the ones who may have left no clues, no signs, no way to intercede. These are the ones who could not find their way out.

And I also understand a person who is terminally ill, suffering with pain, ready to be released. Their right to choose a time to end their life has its place.

But many suicides are impulsive, a desperate act of escape - to be free of temporary pain. A fleeting overwhelming of the psyche. Often, it's during these crises that the choice is made. If the person can get through the crisis, there's relief that their life was saved. That's why the most important part of a therapeutic relationship is the ability to engender hope. We must be able to provide the lifeline of our hope to one who has no hope, to be able to assure that whatever it is, it will get better. There will be life to live after. If I didn't believe that, if I was unable to offer that hope, I wouldn't have been a successful therapist.

I've seen too many lives lost, and I've comforted too many broken hearts left with only unanswered questions. I believe death by suicide is the single most selfish act a person is capable of. I can't tell you that this is a clinician talking, an adult woman talking, or the little girl in me who couldn't save her parents. It's likely a combination of the three. Even though I know that sometimes all doors seem closed for a person in mortal pian, my first gut level response is anger. While that sounds like I'm judging, I'm not. This isn't about judgement. It's about the wounded survivors left to suffer. Yet, I also know unless we've been in those shoes it's hard to say what we would do. All I know is I'm thankful for every person I worked with who chose their life, their future, and their people. I never heard anyone say they wish they had died. Not once.

If your person suicides, you, the survivor, are left with your grief and the questions. You must move forward in an uncertain world, a world of clouds and confusion without closure. If a suicide note is left, there will be a few questions answered – the why now and maybe reassurances that you're not to blame. But a note won't offer you peace. It won't satisfy your questions. It won't relieve you of the unbearable guilt and self-blame that you should have known, you should've saved her. Why didn't you call? Why did you call? Why didn't you stop by? Why did you stop by? Was it the words you said? Was it the words you didn't say? The razor-sharp questions will slash at your heart and your soul. It'll take months, if not years, to begin to assimilate this loss. Any death by suicide is a complicated grief. Professional help is of great value. I would say it's required. You'll carry, not just the regular stages of grief, but the anger will be rage, the depression will be the bottom of a deep well, and the acceptance will be a long time coming.

But it will come. You'll find your way out of this loss. You'll find some legacy for your loved one.

The inevitable blame you place on yourself will quiet most days. The "if onlys" find their place in the recesses of lost time. And the forgiveness of your loved one who voluntarily left you will drift into your heart after many months of refusing to look its way. Holding on to your anger offers strength against the pain of your heartbreak and the ravaging of your soul. But it will, at some point, not be needed any longer and you'll find resolution in forgiveness.

Suicide is an uncomfortable topic. Most of us have conflicting feelings. Have you ever had suicidal thoughts or attempted a suicide? Have you gotten help? Are you happy to be alive?

Have you had a loved one attempt or complete a suicide? It's important to take a minute and process your feelings. Journal. Make calls if you need to.

This is the moment that I tell you if you are having any serious suicidal thoughts, please tell someone. Get help. This is also the time that I tell your friends, your family – if you're worried that your loved one is thinking of suicide – ask, share your worries, assist them in getting help.

Loss of self

Many life circumstances cause sorrow - the loss of a dream, a job, an identity. It could be the loss of health or loss of youth. We grieve. This chapter is a bit scattered as we cover a lot with few examples. I spend a lot of time on the loss of health and aging because that is personal to me. It's also been one of my favorite soapboxes. There's a lot we can do to age positively, even in the case of illness or other limitation. You'll find resources and guidance to help you process these often-inevitable shifts in life in the toolbox section.

Loss of dreams

What if you have a dream since childhood to be a doctor? For as long as you remember, it's been the answer to "What do you want to be when you grow up?" It became a part of your identity. Each Christmas and birthday you received gifts that had reference to medicine – a toy doctor bag with all the accoutrements, a microscope, books on the traits of a good physician. You took all the right classes, volunteered appropriately, and got into a good premed program. It was a foregone conclusion that you were going to make a great doctor.

However, you were not a stellar student, and hard as you tried, you couldn't pass the MCAT exam. You couldn't get accepted to a medical school. You realized you weren't going to be a physician. Your dream was lost. With it went a part of your identity. You grieved that loss. There was sadness and disappointment as you struggled to accept this truth. You became a paramedic and went on to have a fulfilling career, saving many. But it took a process of grief to come to healing. And even today there are pinpricks to your heart and pride whenever you're reminded of this loss.

This sort of sorrow applies to anything we dream big about and find the lifelong goal unattainable. We're taught that you can do anything if you put your mind to it. That's a very inspiring statement. There are many times in life it's true. But it comes with a double-edged sword as some goals are, in fact, not achievable. There are physical or mental limitations that can't be overcome. Like the doctor dream, some must be given up or get transitioned to a plan B. The feelings of loss need to be dealt with.

Parents and families are called to face a loss of dreams if a child is born with special needs. We have visions of what our children will become, even while in the womb. When our precious baby is born with a developmental disability, there's a period of adjustment, a reckoning of grief before acquiring strength you never knew you had, as you take on this new reality. Most parents confronted with this loss become super-moms and dads. Whatever the challenge and commitment it requires, the parents without question become the people who can do it. They learn all the ins and outs of assistance. They learn to go without sleep. They learn to adjust their concept of normal family time. The transition almost seems so flawless from the outside, we might forget the hours and days of anguish of the initial news and the chronic grief that goes with their days – forever.

What if a child full of promise, a high achiever, a joy to his family begins the slow descent into addiction? Where is a parent to go with that sorrow, that fear, that helplessness? Dreams are dashed as reality hits. How long before your hope for recovery begins to feel like wishful thinking? How much pain before you hand the journey over to him? Will you enable, or hand out tough love? Both are fraught with anguish. Help is available from so many sources. Access what you need. Let others help you carry your pain.

Loss of identity

It's not just our dreams that create our identity. We also define ourselves by the work we do. Think about social conversations when you're getting to know someone. One of the first questions asked is "What do you do?" When you get together with friends or family, an early question is "How's work going?" Whether you work outside the home or are a stay-at-home parent, the time you put into that chosen path is significant and generally outweighs your leisure time. But what happens if you've been downsized, let go, or fired? This is loss. This is grief. You ask yourself who you are, and you feel sad and afraid of the future. It takes time to process what this loss means to you. If this change causes financial strain or relationship stress, it produces more anxiety. It's important to take time to heal, to acknowledge your loss, and explore healthy ways to move on.

What about those moms who dedicate their life to caring for their children? There may have been a profession prior to childbearing, but after the first child is born her chosen profession was being a stay-at-home mom. She immersed herself into raising them and homeschooling her flock. It gave her joy and purpose. Then the last one leaves home. She has completed this active phase of her life work successfully. The rooms are now too quiet. The house is too neat. Her heart is broken. It takes time for her to find other means of living a full life – time to process her loss.

Retirement

Retirement is seen as a rite of passage, perhaps the final one before death. It's a time of celebration, a time we anticipate with eager anticipation. Thoughts of that freedom from a work week and its obligations get us through rough times at our jobs. We'll get to relax, do what we want, create our own schedule. All this is true, and it is nice to have that freedom, but who are you now? You're left with the stories of when I worked at ___, or the glory stories of being a ____. To fully move into this new phase, you must first let go of that old identity of your work or recreate it in such a way that it can be incorporated into your new lifestyle. For example, I now had time to focus on writing, and was able to use my past work life as a source for books and essays. Even with that natural transition, there was grief and adjustment to no longer having my identity as a therapist, a role that meant a great deal to my self-view.

According to Erikson's Theory of Psychosocial Development, we now enter his eighth stage – integrity vs despair. This is a critical life transition, a time of reflection. We look back on the life we've lived to tally the pluses and the minuses. With retirement you leave behind stress and pressure. But you also leave behind the most impactful time of your life, the stage where you're most engaged in society. We're the movers and shakers during our middle years. Most of us were productive contributors to society and community, settled in careers, lifestyle patterns, raising a family, and dreaming of retirement.[31]

After leaving work, we reflect on what we've achieved, hopefully the good outweighing the bad. This leads to a sense of integrity and wisdom – the positive side of this stage. You believe you've done your best. But you might dwell on shortcomings or perceived failures. This leads to the negative side – despair and regret. As you process your sorrow of leaving work, you'll hopefully find peace and contentment, not despair.

You can do more now that you have this freedom. As clients began to consider retirement, we laughed at the question – "What do you want to be when you grow up?" You can start new things. It's important to stay curious and engaged in your community, family, and friends.

I witnessed this in action when we moved to a beach town after my husband retired. It wasn't a retirement community, but many residents were in that phase of life. I realized no one asked what I did, and I never heard conversations about work. These folks had fully let go of that era and embraced the next. During the time we lived there, I socialized with people filled with integrity and wisdom. I never did find out what some of them did in their "life before." They'd arrived at the destination of resolution. They let go of old self-views and created new. Their new place was certainly a lot of fun. I learned a lot about life after retirement from these friends who had arrived before me, living their lives with anticipation, engagement, activity, and lots of laughter.

Loss of health

Looking forward to new beginnings implies you're in good health. But what if this isn't the case? What if your future holds medical challenges? There's a natural segue from retirement to these questions, but loss of health can occur at any time.

The young outdoorsman whose professional career reflects his interests has an accident that paralyses him. This abrupt physical change is traumatizing. How can he go on living in this new body? Or what about the young woman who delayed having children, only to be diagnosed with ovarian cancer, losing her ability to conceive. Scenarios such as these change lives forever. The loss is mourned. Emotional healing is needed as well as physical.

Health issues can hit at any stage of life. It might be more dramatic when it's a younger person but not less sorrowful. What about the new retiree who's taken sailing lessons and purchased his boat for the trip he and his wife planned? That journey never happens because he has a massive heart attack, or his wife has a stroke. What about the retired professor whose dream is to mentor underprivileged teens, only to be diagnosed with Alzheimer's Disease? These are examples of loss - loss of identity, loss of health, loss of dreams. It's important to face these feelings. In doing so, you'll find a path to healing and embrace what's left behind.

Loss of youth

In his book *I Asked for Wonder*, Abraham Heschel reflects on our cultural view of aging and its inaccuracies. "Old age is something we are all anxious to attain. However, once attained we consider it a defeat, a form of capital punishment." Heschel goes on to say we should be viewing it differently. "Old age is not a defeat but a victory, not a punishment but a privilege." [32]

When I was a nursing student, I had an elderly lady as my patient. She was recovering from a broken hip. She was feisty, cheerful, and engaging. She talked about all the changes she'd seen in her body and agility over the years, laughing about jars she couldn't open, shoes she couldn't bend over to tie, sagging skin that jiggled when she wore sleeveless dresses. She ran a list of sad/funny stories of lost vigor, bad feet, neck wrinkles, uncomfortable bras, dying friends, icy sidewalks, and lost tastebuds.

But she ended with a positive every time. I commented that she seemed to be doing well considering she was ninety-three and still lived on her own. She laughed and crinkled the wrinkles around her still sparkly blue eyes, and said, "But honey, I'm still eighteen inside!" Peering in, I saw that giggling teenage girl, curious, naughty, excited for what comes next. Her steady gaze still ready for adventure. I laughed with her because I thought she was a cutie.

At twenty-something, I couldn't understand. As my life moves on from young student to aging adult, I now know there's never been a truer statement than the one that sweet lady shared. I'm not ninety-three, but I've become better acquainted with the changes that occur with age. I used to be one who thought age was a state of mind. If I thought young, I'd stay young. I still believe attitude has a lot to do with it, but we can't stop the body from changing in ways that dear lady described. Thinking young with a positive outlook helps us cope more successfully though and likely slows decline. We can't stay young forever. But by navigating the challenges, losses, and transitions, we can keep that youthful attitude.

Before my sixty-fifth birthday, I attended a writer's retreat on Ossabaw Island, Georgia, where I recommitted to writing. On my birthday soon after, we attended "Whisper and Shout," a local spoken poetry night frequented by young poets. They welcomed me with bumper music of "Brick House" and cheered me on as I read my poem I'd written about age. I enjoyed celebrating my years and taking new risks.

Recently, I've discovered another inspiring person. In her eighties, Margareta Magnussen became a writer, after years as an artist. Her first book, *The Gentle Art of Swedish Death Cleaning*, inspired millions to get through the clutter of their lives and not leave this task to others after we die. Her second book is *The Swedish Art of Aging Exuberantly: Life Wisdom from Someone Who Will (Probably) Die Before You*. In this book of autobiographical essays, she reminisces her life as a world traveler, artist, wife, and mother of five. It's a realistic look at aging, the things we lose and the things we gain. She offers practical advice about maintaining social contact, doing what you enjoy, and how to treat others. In a chapter titled, Don't Fall Over and Other Practical Tips for Graceful Aging, she offers a clear-eyed look at what happens to an older person when they fall.

She sums up the realities with "Aging is often difficult, but it doesn't have to be if you approach it in a way that isn't too filled with drama or with dread. And if you can find a way to make aging itself into an art, where you are creative in how you approach each day, perhaps it can be a little easier."[33]

But like everything, there are other sides to that story. Some of us don't maintain the positive attitude of my ninety-three-year-old mentor or my new hero, Margareta. We assume we'll get sick, take multiple prescriptions, and get swallowed up in a drug plan donut hole. We have an ache, and we quit moving. We quit moving, we ache more. We feel depressed as we sit around all day, and ache even more. We quit cooking and socializing, golfing, and gardening. We forget we're created to be healthy. We forget we have a degree of control. I once had a poster with an elderly lady holding herself horizontal on parallel bars. The poster read – "If you rest, you rust." Point taken.

The body works hard to maintain balance, but we must do our part. Aging doesn't have to mean illness or disability. No one's going to live forever. Accepting that is a key to good mental health. But why not live your best life until then? Sometimes we must learn to live with a chronic disease, disability or battle a life-threatening illness. If we have a strong body and a positive attitude in place, it increases our ability to cope and recover.

When illness hits

I like to think my recent cancer journey went well partly because of healthy habits and optimistic outlook. At the same time, I wracked my brain trying to figure out what I did wrong, how I let it happen. I'd spend days beating myself up for the post-menopause increase in my weight and waist. I felt guilty that I drank red wine. I had a need for control – anything that I could do to prevent this from happening again. Regrettably, my oncologist told me my greatest risk factor was I was seventy. This left me in a state of anxiety. I became a fanatic about any potential carcinogen. But slowly, I dealt with my fear. I still eat healthy and exercise regularly, more often than not. Due to a medication I'm taking to prevent cancer recurrence my metabolism is pretty much non-existent, so weight loss is nominal. But I have moved into a phase of acceptance. I have a mild case of nerves a few days before my biannual oncology appointments and mammograms, but other than that, I live my life with less fear.

Honestly, when I got the call about the need for a repeat mammogram that day, there was a sense of the inevitable. It was 2020 after all, why not cancer in the middle of a pandemic? My mother had been a two-time breast cancer survivor, as well as an aunt. I had two other events of abnormal tests in the last twenty years, both of which revealed no cancer, but increased risk factors. I felt there was a bit of a ticking time bomb in my breasts. I was fortunate that my lumpectomy had clear margins and negative lymph nodes along with all the other letters and abbreviations that defined a good prognosis. Chemotherapy wasn't required. A few weeks of radiation was doable.

I learned so much from the beautiful warrior women I met in the radiation waiting room. We sat in a twelve-by-twelve room each day in patient gowns and pandemic masks, a sorority of hopeful eyes and positive words. The stories from these heroes got me through. I hope there were days I helped carry their burden also.

The grace of the young woman, bald and pale, who came in each day in her boho skirts and smiles, stretched my heart to its capacity for empathy. She never told us what her treatment was for, and you don't ask if someone doesn't volunteer – radiation waiting room etiquette. The wife who waited for her husband, he an invalid from a stroke and recently diagnosed with lung cancer, who talked of the plans they had before their life changed forever, but not one whine or hint of self-pity. Then the woman about my age going through her second time around. She said they got it all after chemo and radiation two years ago, only to find that her gone cancer had metastasized to her lungs, bones, and brain since her last six-month check. She talked matter-of-factly of all the reasons she would like to live longer – her son and her grandson who was just starting high school, and her dog, Ralphie, her best buddy since widowed ten years ago. But she said she's lived a good life and if it's time to go, well…. There was a woman in her fifties, also with breast cancer, who had just fallen in love again after a divorce years ago, not willing to think about the future now. She said it's too scary to plan.

There's a bell that you ring when radiation is completed to celebrate the end. My husband rang his bell in Savannah, Georgia years ago following radiation for prostate cancer. All his caregivers gathered around and cheered. It was quite moving for both of us. In the time of pandemic radiation, there was no bell to ring. It was covered in plastic as a covid precaution. I finished my last treatment, dressed, and left. I somehow felt unfinished, left with a sense of limbo. If there's no celebration, is it over?

Once my radiation area was healed and I got adjusted to taking a pill every morning, I was able to physically put the experience behind me. The ladies of my waiting room sorority stay with me in my heart. I'm more vulnerable as I face the reality that my body is not indestructible. The recommitment to living every moment as if it's my last has diminished a bit with the passing of time. But my level of gratitude continues at a higher level than before. I've gone on with life and found the threads to weave these events into my history. What will happen if it comes back? I don't know. I had a scare six months ago when they called me back for another film. It turned out to be some artifact or skin fold or whatever – not another assault on my breast and my being. Like any grief, there are times it hits me. Oh my God, I've had cancer! And there's a visceral shiver of fear that it'll return, cloaked in indigestion, headache, or backache, symptoms we don't immediately react to. It'll be awful, and I know I'll die. Fear overtakes me. I cry for all I'll miss. I'll curse myself that I didn't start my family earlier. I'll let it all wash over me. Then, I dry my tears and thank God I'm healthy, add a prayer for prevention, and go on about my day as a survivor.

It takes time to adjust to any life change. Validate this as a loss. Let yourself grieve. There'll be new challenges to face, skills to learn, and twists you didn't anticipate. It'll make you sad and angry. You'll tumble back and forth in the grief stages. There will be "Why me?" Then comes the real question, "Why not me?" You'll find peace only to have it ruffled up, and tossed around in tumult. This kind of grief is fluid. There isn't a moment of finality like death. There's a slow, dawning awareness that this is here and it's going to keep coming. Adjustments and learning curves will be met head on. You'll have courage you didn't know you possessed. No matter what the physical change, you'll meet it and slowly embrace it as a part of your new reality.

Have you experienced any of these kinds of losses? How did you cope? How did you find resolution? Take time to make some notes in your journal.

When you know you're dying

My weeks in the radiation waiting room taught me much about the human capacity for courage in light of illness. Placed in a previously unthinkable situation, the brain rages, and the heart grieves, but we rise to the new challenge with strength and grit.

In my research for *Surviving Grief*, I read books about the death of a loved one or going through a divorce or an illness. Some were children's books. There were also memoirs written by people who had a terminal diagnosis. These carry the reader through the last days of living. Some were completed by a loved one, as the author died before finishing.

One of these was *When Breath Becomes Air* by Paul Kalanithi, a young physician faced with a Stage IV lung cancer diagnosis. In his book, he struggled to find balance between being the doctor who healed and the patient who was going to die. His wife Lucy finished this book after Paul's death. She recounts how difficult the last few years had been, but she writes that "they have also been the most beautiful and profound of my life, requiring the daily acts of holding life and death, joy and pain in balance and exploring new depths of gratitude and love."[34]

Tallu Schuyler Quinn was terminally ill with a brain tumor when she wrote *What We Wish Were True*. In pondering her imminent death, she wrote "We are fleeting, stunning, song-filled, tender, determined, strung together into an imperfect but woven whole. We are the trillium, spicebush, monarch, turtle shell, fire ant, wild dogwood, redbud, mayapple, goldenseal, bluebell. And the ephemeral larkspur, who's incredible strength is like our fleeting, willful, miraculous lives. You show us how to live. You show us how to die. Can you show us the way beyond death?"[35]

I'll hold on to the incredibly bittersweet beauty of these grief stories. I hold a somewhat mystical view of death; I carry a sense of awe of one who knows they're going to die. What I'm most touched by is how the burden of impending death weaves its way into everyday life. There's purity in the chronic anticipatory sorrow. All they'll leave behind is touched and laid back down. There's a tenderness to the ordinary, gratitude for every breath. Life goes on and fuses the treatment, pain, separation, fear along the path into the activities of living.

As we accept impending death, it gives us an opportunity to make amends, to face our regrets, broken relationships, lost chances. There comes a clarity of what's meaningful, what's worth holding on to. A settling of accounts. A peaceful pulsing sadness beats with the heart, but life continues as long as that rhythm persists.

Dascher Keltner, in his book *Awe*, cites "life and death as the seventh wonder of life…We are awestruck by how, in an instant, life comes out of the womb. And on the other end of the life-death cycle, when a person makes the transition from being a breathing physical being to some other form of existence."[36]

We've all quietly pondered our own end. There may be late night discussions or thoughts of "if you could choose." Would you want to know you're going to die? Would you prefer a sudden death? Or time to prepare and say good-bye? Of course, there isn't an end-of-life menu where we get to select. None of us knows when that time will come or in what form. But we still sometimes pretend that we get to choose.

I've selected age 96-106. But I want to be in age-appropriate good health and of sound mind until the end. By that age there'd be ample time to say my good-byes and prepare for death. In my Sixty-Five Jive poem (Appendix A) I spoke of trailing off in a front porch rocker. Later I hoped that, on the day of my death, I would work in my garden and sit on my porch swing with an old friend. I envisioned petting my cat (though I don't presently have one) and drinking lemonade during a perfect late summer day. That evening I'd have dinner with my family, and that night I'd die in my sleep.

But as I age, I envision dying in a sunlit room on a beautiful day. My family is surrounding me, talking softly, holding my hands, with background melodies of children's whispers and occasional bursts of giggles. My pets will lay on my feet, and there'll be soft music that I love and scents that calm me. The soft breeze will rustle the leaves and the windchimes will offer a sound bath. I'll feel peace and begin to get glimpses of light as I see Matthew and the others I've loved awaiting my transition.

"I hope death is like being carried to your bedroom when you were a child and fell asleep on the couch during a family party. I hope you can hear the laughter from the next room."[37] – a lovely quote whose source I've been unable to track, but perfect for this space.

What have you selected from the fantasy "how you get to die" menu? Have you been with someone who experienced a beautiful death? If so, I hope it brought you comfort. But we all have fears. What do you fear? I fear sudden death. Perhaps that's a result of having experienced shocking losses. I don't want to do that to my family and friends – or myself. I want a bit of time to say good-bye. I've been blessed to be with my mother and grandparents near or at the time of their death. I watched two of them pass as I held their hands, sensing when their soul left the physical body. I want my people to sense my soul's whispered release, to feel the essence of my life transcend – to be a part of the mystery.

Take time to think about these questions and write an entry in your journal.

The Avett Brothers wrote a song titled "No Hard Feelings." I expect it reflects their own late-night musings on mortality. The beautiful lyrics contemplate saying good-bye and one's readiness to leave this earth. They ask:

These words carry a sense of the practical reality of death. We do leave our keys and our rings and our coffeepot and our houseplants. Our collectibles, the good dishes, the favorite chair. The pottery dish filled with rocks and feathers and other grandchildren treasures. All we love, left behind. We give our last kisses and hugs. We let go. We leave and never physically return. We put aside the everyday as we lay our heads down for the last time, knowing the next journey awaits. Will we be ready?

Divorce and other relationship fractures

Another life-changing experience is the loss of a relationship. In this chapter, I'll share my grief story of divorce, as well as thoughts on marriage, commitment, and couples counseling. I'll explore factors that impact how deep of a loss divorce will be, and steps to assist with healing. Grief from divorce is confusing and complicated because of the mix of feelings – love, hate, hurt, anger - all focused on someone still living.

I believe in marriage and the commitment it takes to sustain it. Commitment is another onomatopoetic word. It sounds heavy and plodding. It isn't a word that lightly rolls off your tongue like laughter, love, or flower. It just sits there like a big rock with no intention of moving. There's a stubbornness to it, a tenacity without the thrill of challenge.

It's interesting then that a feeling as joyous as love requires a plodding rock to anchor it. But, once the infatuation phase of love begins to wane, the relationship must be able to transition into the real world where anchors are necessary. There, in the harshness of the sun, we don't measure up to scrutiny as well as in the romantic shadows of candlelight. The thrill and exhilaration of new love can be eclipsed by laundry, bills, and crises. Trouble can begin here and grow until even the anchor of commitment no longer holds.

There is also the marriage that is dangerous, emotionally and physically, due to abuse, active addiction, or persistent infidelity. This is not a sustainable or fixable relationship. It should be abandoned as soon as this becomes apparent. It goes way beyond arguing over a bill. Get out. Don't let the weight of commitment keep you in an unhealthy union.

But for most marriages it's about expectation. Marriage isn't constant bliss. It isn't all walks in the moonlight and breakfasts in bed. If life were awhirl with romance, there wouldn't be words like commitment – or divorce.

A relationship becomes a kind of living organism. It has shape and form. It grows and changes, depending on its caretakers and environment.

As an example, look at any houseplant – one that hasn't been watered or doesn't get enough light. It looks different than when you received it – lush, and full of promise. But if there is the teensiest bit of life left in the root of that plant, there's a chance you can revive it. Saving it will take daily work. You'll have to check the soil, turn it to the right light, fertilize, and water. But sometimes, even with the best efforts to restore it, it might be too late, and the plant dies.

It's the same with marriage. You'll do regular maintenance. You'll tend it, pamper it, check it for bugs. There will be times when it may get dry, wilt a little, or develop unattractive spots. You'll do the work to revive it. It could return to its full bloom. Yet, like the houseplant, your best efforts aren't always enough. Sometimes, even with love and care, it dies. Sometimes you must let go.

I respect marriage and its value to society and mental health. My attitude toward the institution is impacted by the vastly different decades of my formative years. I have the affliction or advantage (depends on the day!) of spending my first ten years in the fifties and my preteens and teens in the sixties. While offering a multitude of perspectives, the values of these two decades often collide. The institution of marriage is one of those collisions.

Today, the divorce rate is dropping – good news. One of the main reasons that rate is dropping is that the marriage rate is dropping. Cultural shifts have created a society that no longer requires marriage. Prior to that, you got married. It's what you did. The rare single woman or man stood out and was often the subject of unjust speculation. The good news is that people who get married today want to get married. It's no longer something you must do to be seen as well-adjusted. Women no longer go to college to "find a man," or give up their education when they do, (i.e. me in 1970 – another grief story). The natural fall in the divorce rate reflects this shift. There's freedom to stay single, to divorce, to be a single parent, to live alone. Children of single parents, or same sex partnerships are no longer rare, creating less stress for the offspring. The benefits of marriage are no longer as obvious, although statistics continue to show that married people live longer. With these cultural changes, you'd think that divorce would also be less painful. That isn't the case, and it's why divorce grief is included in this book.

Couples therapy

Before going any further, let's look at marriage and efforts to save it. My priority was saving partnerships, but I also helped many heal as they went through the trauma and sorrow of divorce.

Couples therapy was a favorite part of my work. I spent many hours assisting partners through the travails of conflict and, hopefully, it's resolution. Engaged, newlyweds, seniors, LGBTQ partners all had their time in my office. I commend all of you who took this courageous step and made the effort. Whether you saved a marriage or not, you did the work. If your coupledom ended in divorce, you knew you tried. You honored what was and walked away with sorrow, but also self-respect.

No matter the situation, the first of these sessions revealed a lot. Even in the first five minutes, there was nonverbal communication providing clues. Who sat where? Were they together in the middle of my couch, at separate ends, one on the couch and the other in a chair that sat up a little higher? What partner shook my hand, chatted on the way to the office? Who started the story of why they were there? How was their eye contact? Who interrupted who? Which one crossed their legs, their arms, or turned their heads to their partner, but their bodies turned away? I could frequently sense who was invested in the work and who was there only to say they'd tried before their pre-planned exit.

We discussed the plan for our work in the first session. After the initial couple meeting, each would have a confidential individual time. We agreed I couldn't bring anything from those meetings back to the couple work without permission. But during the individual session, each partner had the opportunity to reveal their commitment to the relationship, infidelity or temptation, history of abuse, or anything that they didn't want to share with their partner yet. If there was an affair, the person involved was requested to write a letter to the outside person ending the relationship and give it to me to mail. An emotional or physical connection outside of the marriage, new and ripe with excitement, was a therapy death sentence.

After the individual meetings, all sessions were together, and the umbrella of confidentiality included the three of us. Every contact was brought to the sessions. If one partner called me with some report about the other, it was discussed in the next meeting. If I ran into one of them at the store, it was brought up in the session.

In my first meeting with a couple, I made it clear that I believed any marriage could be saved. But it took a hundred fifty percent effort on both their parts for that to happen. Just one of them or a half-hearted attempt would not do it. I was humbled to be a part of the healing of many relationships. There were also the ones that didn't have a chance from the start and many in between.

The happy endings, I hold dear. I respect those who made a serious effort, but in the end chose to end their union. It's not easy to make a choice that feels like failure and portends grief. The courage to finally say it's over, knowing the painful process ahead, is hard work too.

If you end a relationship, many factors play a role in how your grief will manifest. Is the divorce a mutual decision? Are you the leaver or the leavee? Did you leave to be with someone else? Do you still love your partner? Was there warning of trouble or did a partner just walk out, leaving a note or not? Have you both been chronically unhappy for a length of time? Does divorce portend financial hardship? Do you have a good support system? All of these are valid questions that will gauge the impact of a divorce. When your divorce is final you might feel relief. You might feel freed. You might feel excitement. But no matter the circumstances, you will grieve. There'll be regret, sorrow, and second guesses.

After thirty-five years of a committed, second marriage with its normal ups and downs, I still look back and get pinpricks of sorrow over my divorce at twenty-seven. As I share that grief story now, there will still be a few tears.

My divorce

In Appendix A, you'll find an essay I wrote about a confusing night during my divorce that started out a celebration and ended in tears. It offers a glimpse into the energy of multiple emotions that bombard the divorce process, from vindicated to shattered, from liberated to lost – all valid feelings that impact those who embark on this journey.

After two years of college, I married a young man whose birthdate drew a draft lottery number of twenty-one, a guaranteed ticket to the infantry in Vietnam, the conflict that haunted our generation. He chose to enlist to avoid that fate and landed a safe assignment as an information specialist for an Army newspaper. He was stationed in south Florida where we remained for three years. This was my first time away from home, initially homesick and hating it. But I found a job which opened the path that led me to nursing. We made good friends and enjoyed the climate. We saw family a few times a year, until finally it was time to return to the life we'd known – changed with new wisdom and new challenges.

We'd been back to Illinois for six months, settled into jobs and finishing school. It was nice to be part of daily family life once again. It was during this time that I lost my father.

My ex-husband and I were at our closest after Dad's death. He was a wonderful support for me in my grief and as I shouldered my mother's grief. He was also there for Mom, including her in most things we did. He was strong and sensitive. Why then, just two years later, did I file for divorce?

The man I married not only had a low draft lottery number. He also had a tragic flaw - a flaw that it took seven years for me to accept wasn't going away. I had to make a choice. Was I willing to live the rest of my life in the shadow of this flaw that ate away at my self-esteem? Should I learn to live with it and make the best of it? He was, otherwise, a good partner and a good friend. But he could not be faithful. And when he couldn't be faithful – he lied. We went through several crises in our marriage, each time a new beginning after tears, anger, and forgiveness. While living in Florida, we separated for four months, but looked at our return to Illinois as the official new beginning to our commitment. Then it happened again. I found myself with such low self-worth that I knew I couldn't leave then. But I made a vow to myself that when - there was no longer an if – it happened again, I'd be ready. Life went on for another year. I started nursing school, and he finished his degree. We'd been married seven years and still hadn't talked about children. I'm thankful for that. I likely would never have left if there had been children. (Do as I say and not as I do.)

That spring, we were both busy. I didn't notice the initial signs I was normally hypervigilant to – the last-minute phone calls, the changes in plans, the unexplained receipts, the tilt of his head as he lied. Maybe I didn't want to see. But finally, someone called and alerted me to open my eyes. I did, and there it was. I stared it in the face, hands on hips and chin raised determinedly. This time I was ready. I did agree to marriage counseling, but after two sessions the therapist told me he couldn't believe I'd remained in this marriage as long as I had. He said to get out.

I'd spent years preparing so I wasn't shocked my marriage ended. But I was Catholic, and I was stubborn. The church said to never give up, and my hard head refused to accept what I perceived as failure. Though I was the official leaver, I felt he had left me long ago with his infidelity. A lot of my love had died, but I still had love for him. I used to tell clients who stayed and stayed in bad relationships, that they were suffering from "but I looooovvvveee him" syndrome. I taught them that even though we may love someone, that doesn't mean it's healthy for us to be with them. I finally practiced what I preached.

It took time for me to get there. But once my decision was made, after years of ambivalence and retreat, I moved forward resolutely. I used my family's attorney whom I'd known since childhood, who was ready to fire me as a client before we were done. I kept giving in to demands and giving my ex things he had no right to just to get it over. Then, of course, I met someone (another thing I always, unequivocally advised my clients not to do for at least six months), which hastened my desire to be out of this marriage.

So, yes, it shocked me when the tears came, the reminiscing about good times, memories of how we met on the quad at school – him tossing a football with his jock buddies. Me sitting with my hippie friends singing folk songs. I believe that I was the only "love child" on campus who ended up wearing a fraternity pin. We were both passionate about the Vietnam war - just on opposite sides. The night I attended an anti-war march I helped organize and sat at a candlelight vigil, he was with his fraternity brothers voluntarily watching over campus buildings to prevent vandalism. Portending things to come? Who knows? As different as we were, we seemed to respect each other's opinions and could debate for hours. We were both smart and strong.

During the divorce process, I'd find myself idly playing a music box – his twenty-first birthday gift to me. How could this happen? Love doesn't just die. Even when it feels dead, there are embers left. It's with these embers that so many fires could successfully be rebuilt if the work is done. For those of us that are left with plain old embers, they do nothing but nag and needle our heart. So, I grieved for the embers, the remnants of promise, the loss of a dream. I swallowed the smugness of being a couple that made it, exchanging it for the smell of perceived failure. But it was easy to carry the victim role. He had wronged me, fooled around, couldn't keep it in his pants. I had been the perfect wife and it wasn't enough. Over the years, as I became wiser and clearer in my relationship to self, I realized that I too played a role in this fracture. I never left my family and "cleaved" unto him, or however the Bible puts it. I remained enmeshed in my nuclear family and forever Daddy's girl. I hadn't grown up in that way yet, so I didn't know how to demand that level of maturity from him.

A few years after our divorce, my ex contacted me, and we met for a drink. It was a nice talk and good to see that he was doing well, and it didn't hurt that I was looking good and doing well also! At one point we did a little marriage post-mortem. He said that he thought we had a communication break down during the time we were both so busy. I leaned in, patted his hand, smiled, and said, "No, no, no. That isn't what happened. Our marriage broke up because you f— ed around." The end. We both honored that truth with a moment of silence and a hand squeeze.

It feels like grief

What does divorce grief feel like? It feels like grief. Separation of the heart, loss of love – these hurt the same. Something dies. I've heard it questioned that maybe divorce is harder because the person is still around, making it more difficult to find a place to put your grief. If you have children, your grief multiplies exponentially, as you mourn for your children's loss as well as your own.

Divorce grief is also slow, like watching a loved one die day by day. There's the sadness as you begin to see the signs of decline, make the painful decisions, the negotiating of who gets the first house you purchased, the going through the possessions – the little things like the conch shells from the Keys or the antique kerosene lantern from an estate sale, custody of the cat, dismantling the life you built together. One of the saddest moments we shared at the end was taking down our large wooden V and J off the living room wall, each walking away with our own initial hugged to our chests.

Then, it's over and life goes on – different and sad. There's sorrow over the loss of person, marriage, social structure. There's a new identity, a new cohort to become acquainted with, friends to divvy up. One, or both, of you will leave your home, your garden, your neighbors, your partner's family. This is a long, slow process of acute and chronic grief, mixed ironically with relief and excitement.

If the leaving was a shock – if you came home one day and your partner said I don't love you anymore, there's someone else. Or if you came home to a note and an empty closet, these shocks cause trauma that keeps you in acute grief longer.

Divorce grief is as unpredictable and heartbreaking as any other kind of loss. I felt sorrow for a marriage that could have been good, for a marriage that needed more grown-up people to fight for it. A male friend told me at some point during this whole process that after seven years, maybe my ex was getting it out of his system and was ready to be faithful. Maybe he did finally get it right. I couldn't have waited that long. I'd have been an emotional cripple.

So yes, there's a time to fight for your relationship, and there's a time to let it go. In the letting go, you encounter feelings you never anticipate, but most often include Kubler-Ross's five stages. Again, you meander in and out of each with predictable unpredictability. The toolbox section later in the book offers you coping skills and guidance to follow your path to recovery.

If you make the choice to divorce, there are several options of professionals who will help you navigate the legal and emotional maze of accomplishing this task. Please utilize all the resources at your disposal.

Counseling is helpful at any stage of the process. This includes couples counseling when deciding whether to stay together or leave, coparenting counseling, and individual and/or family therapy for you and your children to deal with conflicts that arise during the divorce process and after.

Once you've decided to divorce, another source of support is Focused Forward, a divorce counseling coaching program to assist with the travails of divorce. On her website, divorce coach Katie[39] VandenBerg, says to think of her "as your trail guide. This is your journey, but it's a path I've walked personally and with my clients. I can point out the blind spots. I can help you avoid the cliffs. I have the first aid kit when you are wounded." Divorce coaching offers support and problem solving, but also walks you through the legal maze of the lawyer's office and the court system.

Another helpful organization is Divorce Care, a support group for those who are divorced. The monthly meetings consist of a brief video on a related topic, followed by discussion and social time. While not affiliated with a church, the meetings frequently take place in a church space. This group often becomes a healthy support system for a newly divorced individual. As in all grief, it's helpful to hear from people who have survived the loss.

I offer some words of caution as you progress through grief and healing. One is about moving forward and taking risks with a new relationship. First, wait at least six months to get involved in another relationship. You'll be lonely. You'll feel needy. You'll be tempted. Yes, I did it. No, I shouldn't have. Adding another person to the mix disrupts your entire task of processing the grief of the lost marriage. It left me with work to do later in life, having to face and accept my own role in my marriage's failure to thrive. It was also not healthy for my new relationship. In the abrupt abandonment of my feelings about my divorce, I left much growth potential behind. This resulted in me leaving that new relationship after three years – all because of my own unresolved issues. Get through your stuff when the time is right. Don't carry it on your back and dump it on the next person. When the time comes for you to venture into meeting someone new, be whole and healthy, not still wounded.

When it's the right time for a new relationship, I offer another cautionary note. Be aware if the new love interest tries to snuff out your years that included your marriage. You lived a portion of your life, maybe many years, with your ex. You shared life experiences, sorrows, and joys. You can't erase that. It's interwoven in your life fabric. Don't bore or frighten your new partner by talking constantly about your past life with another, but you should be able to feel okay with sharing a story or a memory without fear of retribution. It should feel safe to follow those occasional threads of memory that include your ex-partner's name.

For the children

This is especially true if you had children in your prior relationship. A new partner should never, in no way, nada, interfere with your coparenting of your children. Giant red flags and sirens should go off if there is any inclination that there will be attempts to stifle or interrupt your functioning parental relationship - with your ex or your children. If a person is not ready to engage one hundred percent in the realities of your life, as a parent and coparent, to love your children, that one is not for you. Don't go "but I loooovvvveee him/her." No one has the right to demand more of your heart than your children or make the blending of families anything less than successful work. The new person is either on that team or is a thing of the past.

Also, for you with children, DO NOT make them choose sides or hear you complaining about your ex – their parent who they also love more than anything in the world. Even if you believe that parent deserves no love, your kids will still love them. Amid our own pain and heartache, children's feelings can get lost.

Whenever I had a couple with children decide to divorce, we shifted our counseling focus to successful coparenting. I reminded them that their relationship would never really end. They needed to find a healthy constructive way to move forward. Notice, I said it would never end. Coparenting doesn't end when a child is eighteen. There are graduations, weddings, baptisms, grandchildren's birthdays. Divorced parents need to find a way to be at the very least, cordial and respectful to each other, and expect the same out of any new partner. Because that is what their children needed, longed for, and deserved at the time of divorce, and will continue to deserve and need for a lifetime.

Children see, hear, and sense much more than we think. They're highly sensitive and intuitive. Talk to them. Listen to their fears. Answer their questions. Their feelings deserve validation and a listening ear. They are not a reason for you to decide to stay in a bad marriage. Staying married "for the kids" never ended well for the couple – or their children.

Research shows that a divorce is traumatic for children, but if life gets better following the divorce, like their parents being happier and less arguing and tension, they heal more completely. This, in turn, helps you to heal more completely.

You'll find an essay excerpt and poem in Appendix A written for the children. I include these as a compilation of the thoughts, fears, and questions I heard in my practice – both from children and from adults processing childhood memories. Hopefully, their words will better prepare you for the questions and conversations that might come up at your house as your children process this shift in their life. They're not meant as judgement or preaching, but a testament to how complicated and devastating divorce grief really is for all of you. If you've gone through divorce, or trying to parent post-divorce, or are a child of divorce, please take some time to journal about this significant loss.

How divorce is navigated by both parents, and any others brought into the relationship, portends the future of your children's emotional mental health and their level of resilience in recovering. With love, validation, and trust, children can recover and thrive. Their adjustment will also ease your own transition into your post-divorce life.

I write these words about the children and preach them like it's a given everyone will listen to me and do what I say. Sadly, there are divorcing parents who never achieve this and create a life of chronic misery for themselves and their offspring. It's confounded when one parent is trying to achieve a divorce with less trauma and strongly desires to coparent effectively, but the other partner stays stuck in bitterness and pettiness of their own narcissism, continuing to sabotage their partner at every turn. Unless drastic circumstances exist, you aren't allowed to walk away from this person or deny them contact with their children. They remain a toxic interloper in your life and the lives of the children. This sets up a chronic grief for you as a parent and your kids, complicating and clouding your future.

You can't control this other person's behavior. But utilizing the tools in later chapters will be helpful in coping with this chronic sorrow. Also, please try family counseling. If you're lucky it might be court mandated. Counseling will be helpful for your children to help them cope with their acting out parent. Also seek support for yourself because, as hard as you try, there might not be a successful outcome. An uncooperative ex may be the new reality, setting you up for ongoing grief. A counselor can help you navigate this unpredictable future with skills you will need.

I was not a child of divorce, but I grew up with constant threats that left me with a sense of the temporary. My parents' relationship was stormy enough to instill chronic fear of divorce. My mother always seemed to have one foot out the door. We left many times, me packing my little square white overnight case, to Grandma's house. Generally, we were back the next day. I the only child, center of the universe, felt responsible to hold my parents together. I was their counselor long before I knew what a counselor was. They loved each other madly, and there were many good times. Sadly, they both carried emotional baggage and couldn't hold on to the trust that makes all the difference. I remember, as a small child, my nightly prayers of "Now I lay me down to sleep…always ended with "Please Jesus, don't let Mommy and Daddy get a divorce." Would I have been better off if they had finally divorced? Who knows? We all experienced a sort of anticipatory grief through the years.

My parents certainly would've benefitted from counseling as would any of you who may be considering divorce. Give it a try. See what you discover. A marriage really is worth saving if it's possible. If it isn't, you can avoid the grief and guilt of not having tried. And you'll be better prepared for a future together or alone having worked through the issues causing you pain.

The loss of a pet

You've likely heard that dogs don't live as long because they have less to learn about love than humans do. We nod our head as we read this and smile because we know it's true. Dogs, and our other pets, love so freely, so unconditionally, so purely. And, oh, that sorrow when they leave us.

The absence of a dog or a cat who has been a part of the family for years leaves an empty space in hearts and homes. A young pet who is tragically taken leaves us in shock and grief. A pet who died due to something we did or didn't do haunts us.

Sometimes, it's the painful decision of when it's time to let go. For pets, we have that honor and responsibility to judge when their quality of life is such that it's time to say good-bye. We put aside issues of the extra care an elderly pet requires due to their condition. The focus needs to be on what life is like for your pet. Does he have an incurable disease? Is she in pain? Can he still walk? Is she in control of bodily functions? Does he eat and drink normally? Does she play? Does she still like to cuddle with you? The answers to these questions and recommendations from your vet will help with the decision. The choice to euthanize, to put your pet to sleep, should be a family discussion. If there are children, it's important for them to understand that this isn't a decision made lightly, and that time was taken to think about options and alternatives. Whoever in the family wants to be a part of this good-bye should be allowed to do so. Whether in the vet's office or at home, it can be a tender and gentle act of love. It's heartbreaking and sad, but of value to the hearts who loved him. It gives your beloved pet loving eyes to gaze into as he closes his for the last time.

We're at a family place right now, where we've been blessed with pets that have lived long lives, meaning we and our children's families are facing that decision not too far down the line.

Last year we said good-bye to a valued family member, my son's family's old baby, Cash, a yellow lab mix whose been in our lives forever it seems. At thirteen, he struggled to get off and up on his favorite napping spot. His hind legs quivered and collapsed more than they walked, and he was having other physical issues. The family planned to say good-bye and talked about it in the days before the scheduled appointment. Cashie got ice cream, extra treats, and constant hugs and kisses. His extended family came to say good-bye. I loved on him while heaping his tongue with peanut butter treats. Old pictures of Cash in his prime were reminisced over – Cashie in sunglasses, surrounded by babies, jumping for frisbees, guarding a campfire, dressed up in a handmade flowered wreath jauntily tilted on his head and bracelets on his paws. When it was time, the whole family went to the vets. The kids opted to stay in the waiting room after one last hug and whispered, "I love you." My son and daughter-in-law held him and talked to him until he took his last breath. His collar and ashes are now in a place of honor on their bookshelf. Pictures of Cash on the other side of the bridge frequent my grandson's sketch book.

Sometimes the answer to "when is it time" is clear. Sometimes not. My sweet Cairn Terrier, Frodo – yes, Mr. Frodo Baggins because he liked to go on adventures – was likely ready to go long before I was prepared to say good-bye. At nearly eighteen years old, he'd suffered the indignity of incontinence and feeble legs for a time, until I couldn't deny it anymore. If he could've, he would have likely whispered thank you to me as he took his last breath.

But our dear Sophie, sweetest German Shepherd on earth, was a few months past her tenth birthday when an inoperable rectal tumor was discovered. You'd never know she was sick. A fetcher, she continued to take the UPS driver and the mailman off their schedule most days as she insisted they throw the stick she happily provided – over and over and over. And on her last day, before going to the vet, she still laid her well-loved stick at my feet for a few last fetches. For Sophie, it was preventing the suffering that would accompany the inevitable bowel obstruction. As soon as we saw her having any difficulty with going to the bathroom, we knew it was time. But, oh, it was difficult.

We're comforted in these times of hard decisions by the knowledge that our beloved pet lived a long full life - loved and cared for to the end. But what about the tragic loss?

One of the great tragedies of my family's life was the death of our two-year-old pup, Bo. His full name was Beauregard the Junk Yard Dog, a lab/pit bull mix. He ran around our mini farm like a kid, teasing the chickens and guarding the cats. He loved us beyond measure and we him. We lived on a bluff back from a busy road. He never left the peak of the bluff, no matter where we were below or what we were doing. He had a set point, and he always stayed. Except for a dawning October morning when something – a dog, a coyote, who knows – was bothering the cats in the back yard. He bolted after the assailant, over the bluff, down the hill into the road and the path of a truck whose driver was too busy to stop. The other animal made it across. I heard my husband call to Bo to stop and then an agonized "Oh God." I went outside to see him carrying Bo up the hill. We placed him on the patio settee for his dying moments – the settee he laid on to sun himself after a busy day of chasing chickens. I raced in to tell our daughter who was getting ready for school, our only one left at home. She came out in the chilly morning wrapped in a towel, and we all gathered around petting and telling Bo what a good boy he was and how much we loved him. He died minutes later. My husband wrapped him in his blanket and carried him to the truck. He took him to the vet's where he was cremated. We all tried to go to work and school that day but were back home before ten. A time for grief. A time to honor our friend, Bo. His ashes were in our living room till we moved from that property a few years later. Before we left, we scattered them along the grass he ran with the chickens, cats, and kids. I could almost see his joyous smile and his ears flapping in the wind.

I still have dreams occasionally about my six-year-old cat, Cloudy – a sweet big old gal who I accidently shut in the attached garage before bed one night. We found her dead the next morning, probably of a heart attack from stress and fear. Even though it's been years, sometimes, in my dreams, she will still lay on my legs like a warm blanket, and I'll feel her vibrate with purrs. And I tell her I'm sorry.

There was the miracle goldfish named Phish who my daughter rescued at a fall festival from an eight-year-old who was swinging him madly in his clear plastic bag. Phish lived seven years, a record for carnival fish in our family. He was my constant companion as his bowl sat on the kitchen island. We had some great conversations about life. He was found deceased by my husband who was tending to me post-foot surgery. I hadn't been in the kitchen for three days. I hoped he didn't die of a broken heart, thinking I'd abandoned him.

Our bird, Shaquille O'Neil, the Cockatiel, was the first pet our oldest son named. We got him as a birthday gift for my husband. Shaq was only six months old and could already whistle the Andy Griffith theme song. You'd often here him talking to himself or giving us a "Boo" or an "uh oh". His cage was in front of a tv room window so he could keep an eye on the goings on outside. In January, there was a bit of a draft from that old window. We didn't know cockatiels' susceptibility to respiratory infections. We were watching some show and our son pointed out that Shaq sounded hoarse. He soon fell to the bottom of his cage. The emergency vet told us to put him in the bathroom with the shower running – like a baby with croup. But it was too late, and we had to say good-bye. I chastised myself for not thinking about the draft, not keeping him warm enough. We had a memorial service, and Shaq was buried in the back yard flower bed. Unbeknownst to us, his grave was near where Matthew's tree would be planted later that spring. It was the beginning of a very sad year.

None of us has any way of measuring how much one's pet means to them. It can range from those who for some reason have a pet only to be cruel, or dogs whose only function is for hunting, well cared for but little loved, to the widower whose old German Shepherd is his family, lifeline, and most important buddy in this world. There are kitties, dogs, hamsters, gerbils, pigs, ducks, rabbits, fish, turtles, birds, and assorted other amphibians to love and care for and be members of our families. We once had an iguana named Iggy, our Sophie, a cockatiel named Echo, and our sweet old Frodo who hung out together on the couch. All were valued members of the family.

Cloudy's sibling, Edgar left our mini farm one day and never returned. I feared he'd met his demise on the busy road. I told the kids, that until we found otherwise, we'd assume he crossed the ravine and entered the parallel universe on the other side. One day I was walking in the subdivision down the road and here comes a cat that looked like Edgar. I said, "You look like Edgar, a kitty I used to have," and he cocked his head, and came running to me. I picked him up and he put his paws around my neck in a little cat hug, just like Edgar used to do. I cried, "You are Edgar!" and he burrowed his nose in my neck. I felt like the little boy in the Velveteen Rabbit. I checked a couple houses and found out he was now with a lady who had accumulated five cats (one who was one of our missing barn cats). Edgar was fat, happy and had a new home. I told my daughter that night that I found Edgar, and he wasn't in a parallel universe across the ravine. It was on Sheridan Road! We all laughed and cried for Edgar the survivor, who had been a special member of the Mitchell family prior to his most fortunate adoption.

As much as I rail about euphemisms, I cherish the Rainbow Bridge. Our pets deserve to cross into a land of rainbows. There is no human capable of the love, loyalty, and devotion that a pet offers us, especially a dog (my personal bias). There are those who love and trust their dogs more than people. There are many of us whose pet is the most important loved one in our life. Early on I mentioned those who are afraid to get close to others, fearing loss and abandonment. Pet relationships can offer these hearts the chance to love another and be loved without the human entanglement they fear.

Often, the first loss for a child is a pet. Don't place hierarchal value on said pet. A goldfish is just as much a loss to that little heart as the family dog. No turtles or fish or hamsters in the garbage or toilet – unless it's a part of the funeral plan, which your child should have a hand in creating. Do not ever secretly replace a dead pet with a look-alike. You'll tell yourself it's to protect your child's feelings, but you'll know in your heart that it's you you're protecting. So, no. Never do that.

When a pet dies, honor that life. Grieve his loss. Remember him. Our three dogs are now, sixteen, twelve and ten. Though they are all in relatively good health, albeit a little deaf, blind, and slower, I'm aware that the Rainbow Bridge looms in our not-so-distant future. There'll one day be less hair on the blankets and slobber on the furniture. There'll be less trampled flowers in the garden, less sticks to retrieve, and fewer half-eaten tennis balls. But oh, how empty our hearts will be.

Don't forget to add significant pet losses to your timeline. And, please, take a few minutes with your journal to tell your story - honor that rabbit who always took time to listen to your problems, the caged mouse your mother threatened, the infamous rescued carnival goldfish, and the two notorious hamsters named Thunder and Lightning. Remember your first dog, named Queenie, or the painted turtle who watched for you through the glass of his home, bobbing up and down as you entered the room. They were all special. They all deserve honor. They were all love.

A final note – two weeks prior to publication, we said good-bye to our dear Skittles.

She was the head of our household for sixteen and a half years, ruling with love and kisses. Rainbows await, sweet girl. Run free.

Good grief

There are good changes in life that carry loss. Whenever we move forward, we leave something behind. When we grow, we give up a piece of our past. Every growth and positive change are accompanied by a little trail of loss and grief.

You get that job of your dreams that requires relocation. How exciting, - a new beginning and the opportunity for growth. But in doing so, you leave family, friends, home, social structure behind. Any positive and enriching journey we embark on is a welcome one. But don't avoid feelings of sadness when you have the last weekly family dinner, or go to your last book club meeting, or say good-bye to your friends you've known since kindergarten. Something as simple as your last dentist appointment with the guy who did your braces at thirteen, the last visit to the grocery store where you worked as a bagger in high school, or the last coffee at the local restaurant will bring a swell to your heart and tears to your eyes.

As a happily married couple, you're ready for the major change of becoming parents. The excitement of pregnancy, decorating the nursery, the dreams of how it's going to be are forefront in your heart and mind. But there'll be those nights when the two of you are up late, snuggling on the couch, that you'll feel a tiny sadness that these quiet intimate times will soon be far less frequent. Or on the Friday afternoon, when he calls and says pack a bag for a weekend at the beach with friends – childless friends. Or those hot spontaneous sexual encounters in the kitchen, hallway, bathroom – not so much after the children arrive. We give up something to get something. Honor that transition. Value the precious memories, that will be fodder for remember whens.

Or what about when your last child leaves for college – a good thing, right? But oh, the tears that come at the oddest times. Finding a sock under the bed sits you down. Cooking broccoli and not having anyone complain, hearing their favorite song on the radio without a loud vocal accompaniment, having a sink free of dirty dishes. All positive. All healthy. All a natural life transition of parent and child. But there are those bittersweet moments of loss and reminiscence. Honor the memories. Remember your time there. Then be open to this new beginning – your next phase of life that accompanies your child's great adventure.

Good grief. The grief that comes with moving forward. Leaving something behind.

Yes. If you must feel loss and sorrow, this is by far the best kind to experience, but the important message is to feel the feels. Honor that which will soon be a part of your past and the gifts it gave you. Say your good-byes. Tell others what they've meant to you. Commit to maintaining relationships from a long distance. Send notes to your dentist and the manager of the grocery store. Make plans with friends. Set a date for family to visit.

Honor the child your college kid once was. Learn the lyrics to the song and sing it yourself. Have positive closure that keeps a part of your heart deeply connected to this place in your history, even as you physically leave it behind. The golden threads will be forever woven into your life tapestry. At this given moment, who you are is a culmination of every event, every person, every breath you've experienced in your life. Value and embrace it all.

If thoughts of these types of transition come to mind, please open your journal and spend a few minutes.

National grief

I hold a deep faith that humans are essentially good. We want to be that way. We feel our best when we are. In the movie *Starman*, Jeff Bridges played a lovable nineteen-eighties alien. He tells his earthly sidekick that his favorite thing about us is that we're at our best when things are at their worst. Amid personal or communal tragedies, we experience primal moments of goodness. During these times, we're vulnerable and raw. We rise with open and responsive hearts. It's involuntary, like breathing. We huddle together and take care of one another.

Pre-pandemic, this chapter looked different. It was terrorist attacks and assassinations. These catastrophic events in history shaped us as we grieved. We gathered as a community or a nation or a global tribe to mourn.

These are the "Where were you when" moments. I'm old enough to remember, with total recall, the day John F. Kennedy was assassinated. I was in my grade school gym playing volleyball when our principal ran in and shouted that the president had been shot. The next hour, we sat in eighth grade Civics class glued to the transistor radio on our teacher's desk. As Walter Cronkite spoke the dreaded words, we all wept. The nation came to its knees. Time stopped as we sat in front of our black and white television screens, watching the ravaged widow and her babies mourn. In my dawning interest in international affairs, I gave this president full credit for saving us during the Cuban Missile Crisis the year before. He was my hero, and he was dead.

The Kennedy assassination was a piece of the rapid decline of that post WWII Golden Age – that time when America was strong, the leader of the world, and the war to end all wars was over. It didn't take long for that fantasy to unravel, as the sixties became the decade of rage, with race riots, assassinations of Bobby Kennedy and Rev. Martin Luther King Jr – and a new war they called a "conflict" that tore the nation apart.

The next generation's "Where were you when" was the day the towers fell. September 11, 2001, a perfect early fall day, the kind that made you glad to be alive. I'd just dropped off my last kid at school. I turned on the radio as I headed to work. The first plane had hit the World Trade Center, unsure whether an accident. I had an hour before my first client, so I headed back home to watch the news. By the time I got there the second plane had hit, and there were reports of other planes. I stared as the terror unfolded. On my way to work, the towers fell. The air space shut down and the nation stopped. My husband, traveling for work, was stranded on a Marine Corp supply base in Jacksonville, Florida. My sister-in-law was grounded in Washington D.C. where she had been attending a conference. At home, shocked and stunned, we moved through the motions of my son's thirteenth birthday, and our small town's fall festival. We jumped at sirens. We noticed faces that looked different than our own. The silent skies echoed in our heads. We were wounded and vulnerable. The catastrophic events of that day took 2,996 souls. The photos of the missing carried by loved ones on the city streets, makeshift memorials on the sidewalks and fences, the dust and ash-covered first responders - these pictures burned into our brains. The crippled nation and its traumatized people gathered, in person and remotely, for the Yankee Stadium memorial service. We wept for those we lost, and for a nation that was changed forever. As we doubled over in our pain, anger became the strongest emotion. And another war began.

I had the opportunity to see the musical *Come from Away* recently. It's the story of the town in Newfoundland that took in 7,000 passengers from planes unable to land in the United States that day. It brought back the shock, the numbness, the fear, the loss. But also, the huddling together and taking care of each other that is us at our best. Never forget.

Where were you when? How did these events impact you? Who or what did you lose? Take time to reflect on your memories of these or other national grief events. These times of life add another story of the rhythm of trauma, grief, and what healing looks like.

You'll find an excerpt of an op-ed written on the one-year anniversary of 9/11 in Appendix A. In it, I remembered the shock, disbelief and crushing reality of the Tuesday morning when the brilliant blue sky erupted into flame and smoke, forever destroying another layer of American innocence. In rereading this essay, I recalled how we huddled together in a community that only tragedy can create.

Now we've experienced another kind of national and global loss. We've lived through a pandemic and its remaining remnants. This chapter was written over three plus years starting in the spring/summer of 2020 and proceeds through 2022, and beyond, chronicling a time that didn't seem to want to pass into history. Yet, it's only history that will determine how we got through it. There's been contradictory thoughts of how we'll be viewed. Coming together and caring for each other was often the case, but there was also a pitiful amount of division and discourse.

Living through a pandemic was not on anyone's list of possibilities to see in their lives. The toll of this national loss, this unrelenting change, continues to be tallied. What will be the lasting affects – emotionally, economically, culturally? It's already clear that life has altered for anyone touched personally by illness or death. The economic ramifications, supply chain challenges, employment difficulty, hospitality industry changes all continue to unfold. The political fallout continues to leave us shaking our heads. No modern society ever did this before. The efforts at recovery are speculative at best. The educational and social cost to our children is still evolving. No one knows. We continue our efforts to fix what has never been broken. But there's hope. The virus seems to be under control. I'm optimistic the rest will eventually follow.

Looking back to the summer of 2021 COVID, cases were creeping down. Vaccines were becoming available. It was time to venture out. It felt like a ravaging storm had passed. As survivors, we began the hesitant, fearful peering through the cracks of what remained. We emerged from shelter as after a storm. Was everyone safe and accounted for? Was the house still standing? We took stock. Then we moved forward, free to get back to "normal". Yet, as after a storm, a cloud of a particular grayness tightened the chest. The sound of a lazy freight train moving through town dried the throat. A breeze, beyond gentle, prickled the hair on the arms.

It seemed our storm had passed. Yet, for a time we shrank ever so slightly when an acquaintance leaned forward to speak. A poorly covered cough set up an impulse to flee. The removal of a mask to eat that restaurant meal we missed so much became an act of courage. The social time we craved tired us. A large group of people milling about resulted in sensory overload. The immediate plans for a trip to the beach, delayed after second thoughts. Maybe later in the year. These are natural responses to trauma: hypervigilance and vague anxiety. What was once normal took on a veneer of threat. It'll pass as the brain moves away from the fight-or-flight instinct that crisis necessitates.

As we moved out of survival mode, we began to have feelings

– feelings that had been covered in just the right amount of numbness to keep us on autopilot, moving through the days we weren't sure would end.

And so goes the recovery from years of pandemic living. Today, we've mostly recovered from our storm, feeling a sense of normal. We're so excited to see friends and family, to dine at our favorite restaurants, take in a ballgame, a concert, a church service. The thought of traveling evokes a yearning we didn't know we had. Being maskless, which at first felt like a naked vulnerability, is once again routine.

We've lived through a pandemic. A pandemic. Think about it. For hundreds of years beyond this will be known as the Great COVID Pandemic of 2020 and beyond. And we're the survivors.

What did you lose? What do you mourn?

First and foremost, there is the grief of all who lost loved ones to this virus. It took people from us. In a horrible, unthinkable way. Alone, without touch or whispered words. Loved ones were left to grieve without the support of ritual, without community. And we grieved for them. Worldwide, over 6,700,000 lives were lost, and 1,100,000 people have died in the United States.

It eventually touched us all. We may have stayed disease-free or not, but every one of us has a story of a neighbor or friends separated by illness or devastating loss. A family in our neighborhood experienced severe cases that started with an Easter family dinner. Everyone got sick. They eventually recovered after weeks of life-threatening illness, but their story ended with both his parents dying, the family making the painful choice to remove them from ventilators - on the same day. Heart-wrenching grief and trauma.

More than a million souls left this earth in our country alone because of COVID-19. Please take a moment to honor this national heartbreak. Each night we heard the tally of numbers on the news. Every number had a face, a name, a life. They left their imprint on this earth. They had hopes, dreams, hobbies, careers. Many were aged, enjoying retirement, and reflecting on the life they lived. And each of these precious souls left behind people who love them. Loved ones were forced to say good-bye without holding a hand or whispering loving words. They're burdened by the truth that their loved one died alone. They weren't allowed to gently lay by their side or hold a hand as they breathed their last.

It's vital for all of us to honor those who died, to grieve for them and their families. This is not how anyone chooses to die. It isn't how anyone want to say good-by to a loved one. It leaves a vacuum of pain for family members, a space that should've been filled with friends and family surrounding them, bringing food and words, and carrying them through the initial pain. There should've been visitations, wakes, Rosaries, funerals, burial services. There should've been celebrations of life, stories, shared remembrances. Instead, mourners were left alone with their grief, lonely and isolated. This is another example of complicated grief which will roughen the road to healing for those who mourn.

Those caring for the sick and dying made a heroic effort to try to comfort those they lost, but even they were confined head to toe in personal protective equipment - unable to touch, voices muffled behind masks and shields.

Part of my grieving process began during the months of anniversary reflections, starting in early March of 2021: the "year ago this time" statements, laden with memory, ripe with feelings. Our last travel in January 2020 was a precious keepsake of life 'before" - a pressed flower of memory. I recalled my last social outing- the joy of rehearsing with my Morton Civic Chorus. We breathed on each other with abandon as we sang our beautiful music, unaware the world was about to change, that we wouldn't be performing our concerts in May, that some of us would be terribly ill, that someone would die. A couple days after, my grandson's third birthday party was cancelled, just to be cautious. He will still tell you, if asked, that COVID ruined his birthday that year. Then the slow slide into a two-week shutdown that would become an entire year. A pandemic Gilligan's Island "three-hour tour."

I remember my naivete about those two weeks, looking for the silver linings of this disruption. We're being forced to slow down and reconnect with our families. That can't be a bad thing, right? I crocheted an Afghan. Our dining room table was scattered with jigsaw puzzle pieces. I binge- watched *Schitt's Creek* and welcomed laughter till I cried. I read books. I enabled my husband's chocolate chip cookie addiction. We bought a PS4 and played golf. We played board games and card games and drank too much wine.

But then, it went on and on and on. We watched the news, the poignant scene of Italians singing from their balconies, their overwhelmed hospital systems, the makeshift morgues. At first, no, this couldn't happen here. Then slowly it started to dawn on

America. It's coming for us. And come it did.

As the two weeks turned into months, enthusiasm lagged. When the reality hit that our grandkids wouldn't be returning to school that year, there was a weird sense of grandparent sorrow. No spring carnivals, no school programs, no grandparent's day. PTO fundraisers, t-ball, dance – gone.

We were fortunate that all our family lived nearby, so even though we couldn't gather for our family dinners, sleep overs, game nights, we could at least visit from the front porch, later graduating to bonfires in the backyard and picnics in the park. A dear friend, like so many others, went an entire year without seeing her out-of-state daughter and grandchildren. So much separation. So many hugs missed. So much just missed.

Time continued to pass. I took long drives in the country, loudly singing show tunes – likely my way of pandemic screaming. We played lots of games, watched many movies, ate too much home-cooked comfort food, and still drank too much wine. I became one of the sourdough bread makers that emerged as a symbol of pandemic pastimes.

I was thankful every day that we could be outside safely. Solitary walkers, bicyclists, and runners kept a social stream of faces going by our front porch. Daily walks saved the sanity of many, including my own. Those walks were cheered by the soulful sidewalk art of children unable to go to school. Hearts, flowers, words of encouragement all chalked on my path between hopscotch and tic-tac-toe grids. There were signs made by these kiddos to tell us that things would get better and to be kind. One family of ardent Harry Potter fans posted signs with Dumbledore's words of wisdom and encouragement in their yard. And the windows of homes with children – filled with hearts. Yes. We are at our best when things are at their worst.

We made do with new rituals that loosely resembled what we missed. The first time my grandchildren's school did a "teacher parade" around the neighborhood, I stood on my front porch with tears streaming - waving at each decorated vehicle. Teachers and their families leaned out windows with greetings and words of encouragement for their students and families. Their horns honked and music played. They did what they could to stay connected with the kiddos they loved.

Birthday parties took on a similar mobile practice, with the honoree standing or sitting in their yard as streams of decorated cars proclaimed it was a party – a pandemic party.

Local musicians lost in the limbo of COVID began to put on free porch concerts with socially distanced spectators. We were invited to bring lawn chairs and enjoy the talents of these folks whose livelihood was so threatened. But these concerts had nothing to do with money. They represented their need to play, to practice their art and have an audience to enjoy it.

It does our hearts good to do good. Opportunities for volunteer work opened for those at low risk, like handing out food for families and manning food pantries. But so many structured giving habits were disrupted. The volunteers at cancer centers were gone, drivers who picked up the lonely for their chemotherapy, the caregivers who visited with them during their treatments – gone. The folks who brought cheer and nail polish and pampering to nursing homes, the therapy dog handlers – gone. The lonely got lonelier. The meal providers at Ronald McDonald Houses – gone. Homeless shelters, animal shelters. Then there were the museums, the parks, the zoos, all closed – shutting out the multitudes of volunteers who brought and received joy through the services they freely provided. Yet, we had a deep need to give, to connect, to still feel part of the tribe of humanity we so cherish. I learned the favorites of everyone on our block and made cookies for neighbors and friends. We placed cookie-filled paper bags tied with ribbon with marker-drawn hearts, on our neighbors' porches, waving from a distance. We became more passionate donators to food pantries that suddenly became the only food source for many. I gave more money and food to the folks with the signs at intersections.

Public service announcements about everyone sticking together made me cry. Watching healthcare worker interviews made me sob. I remember what working a few days of chaos at the hospital was like. It's impossible to fathom what these caring, sensitive professionals went through, seeing death every hour of every day, unable to comfort, overwhelmed with fatigue, often separated from their own families and support systems. PTSD will be measured for years to come. We don't even know what it will look like yet.

Take a minute and think about what you did different in that first year. How did the pandemic change your life, your schedule, your connections? What did you lose? And what did you learn?

Was your church family disrupted? For thousands, church – not the building but the people in it – is the core of a spiritual, emotional, and social support system. One bleak day in March, we were told to stay home. Like so many other institutions, churches quickly adjusted to the new reality and went fully online for services. This took care of the spiritual needs, but still left many isolated. You lost the pre-church coffee, Sunday School, potlucks, Wednesday night youth activities and Bible studies. You were left adrift. Zoom and streaming maintained a degree of connection, but the coffee chatter, the food made with love, the social home for children was gone.

What about your fitness routine, and all its benefits? While primarily for physical health, the gym is another social structure that was disrupted. For many, the Tuesday-Thursday spin class is a close-knit group whose connection goes beyond the bikes. The swimmers in the laps either side of you become your friends, the weightlifters who spot you, your encouragers. The juice bar was a place to laugh out your endorphins with fellow fitness enthusiasts. Gone. I felt the loss of a Monday-Wednesday "senior" fitness class. I was a relatively new member, but some had been regulars for years. One lady, in her nineties, and her two daughters had come for thirty years. Breakfasts were planned around it. Christmas gifts were exchanged. Rites of passage celebrated. Losses shared. Gone.

There were no in-person senior classes at the local university, no in-person book clubs, card clubs, coffee klatches. All gone.

And what about the experiences the younger people missed? Senior prom, senior skip day, graduation, sports seasons that may have impacted college scholarships. The anticipated markers of maturing, passages of substance for a high schooler lost. They're memories will have great chasms of developmental and social voids.

My friend and fellow author, Holly Peterson, wrote on her Facebook page in December 2020 about her daughter missing her Christmas band concert. "My heart hurts so much. No concerts. No pep band. No Disney trip. No shared giggles for Lucy during band class. No funny stories or embarrassing moments. But as usual, she is tough…So last night when Lucy shared her completed assignment with me, her Christmas duet with herself, recorded and edited to sound like two trumpets playing 'Silent Night', I expressed delight and then I cried. Playing a duet with yourself sums up this year."[40]

Some things I missed surprised me. It's things we don't realize are integrated into life's fabric, but then we see unravelling threads that look like loss. Like standing in line for coffee and chatting with those around you. I yearned to be in a crowded elevator or hurrying along a busy street. My heart ached for a standing room only concert, dinner out in a loud crowded restaurant. What about rushing through a busy airport to catch a connecting flight, with the hum of the world's cultures surrounding you? I missed those moments – the ones I hadn't thought much about before. These are the ones where a brushing of shoulders on a busy street or a jostle on a packed train remind you, you're a part of this crazy human machine. But their absence brought their meaning and worth to the surface of my heart. What did you miss that you didn't know you would?

What about the events you had planned that had to be cancelled?

My heart went out to the brides whose dream wedding was not to be, and the pregnancies and births without the physical support and presence of family. So many milestones that usually called for celebration and community – all either cancelled or done alone.

Along with all the daily routine losses, we had four trips cancelled that summer. We were going to see the Avett Brothers at Red Rocks for three concerts – cancelled. We had a house rented in Wisconsin for a whole family vacation – cancelled. My husband had finally talked me into going to Las Vegas for a show – cancelled. A trip to see old friends at our home away from home – cancelled. It was all just gone.

How did it impact you when the NCAA tournament was cancelled, and the baseball season didn't start? What about the empty stadium football games with cardboard fans and canned cheers? Or the NBA bubble?

Musicians' attempts to play their music tugged at my heart. One of my tear-makers was a Colorado concert to raise money for musician workers in the state. Nathaniel Rateliff sang a lonesome ballad to an empty Red Rocks amphitheater. The Lumineers played a soulful piece to an empty Denver Broncos stadium. Haunting. An annual hometown New Year's Eve concert by the Avetts transitioned to a Zoom performance from their studio. And what about when the lights went out on Broadway? When the plays and musicals were cancelled it took on another level of realness. These were the days the music really did die.

There are some things we might not remember until we sit with this for a bit. Just as they are for me, yours will come rising to the surface. Take time to feel each one, to taste its place on your tongue, to let it rest on your heart. Honor what you lost. Please sit with your journal and think about all the questions scattered throughout this chapter. What stood out for you? What of the questions touched your heart, or misted your eyes? What does moving out of this moment in history feel like to you?

We all lost more than a year. It happened insidiously. We've been like the frog in the pot of water. That March moment, we were placed on the stove and the temperature was slowly turned up - so slowly that we adapted to it. We went on automatic pilot, numbing to the absence of hugs, grocery aisle chats, shoulder-brushing of strangers. You've had your own brand of loss – universal in many ways, yet achingly unique to your life. We tend to minimize our own if we managed to stay relatively comfortable and safe. I struggle with those feelings when I think about how we weathered this storm. My family lives nearby. No one got seriously ill. No one lost jobs. But, like all of you, I have sorrow. It's important to honor it. The pandemic impacted years of your life. Let that soften you, heal you, and leave you a gentler human.

Planetary Grief

Before leaving the topic of national grief, let's address a related subject - grief for the entire planet.

I find myself, a generally positive person, carrying a chronic sense of sadness just on the edge of consciousness. If I quickly turn my head, I catch it head-on and get pulled under in the enormousness of possible catastrophes that await us, and the burden of the daily evidence of man's inhumanity to man. In the age of constant information, it's impossible to stay in denial for long. Bad things are happening in the world. I'm aware there's been corruption, greed, violence, and abuse throughout history, but now my grandchildren have active shooter drills in school. The term 'lockdown' has become part of their vocabulary. We seem to have reached a precipice that we balance precariously on, teetering with unnerving uncertainty.

A friend of mine recently responded to a question about her day, with this surprising statement. "I'm good, other than an overwhelming feeling of sadness and depression over world events and climate change." So, it's not just me being old and a worrier. She's in her forties, raising a family, and passionate about her community and the earth it sits on. I know millions carry this fear, who wonder what will get us first – climate change or war. And wondering what they can do about it besides turning down plastic straws and composting.

As a grandmother, I grieve for my children and grandchildren who look at an uncertain future. Will our planet be habitable in the years ahead? Have we left our heads buried in the sand of complacency too long? Are we beyond the point of turning things around? With many years on this planet, I can't deny the increase in heat, violent weather, wildfires destroying thousands of acres and ecosystems, king tides causing routine flooding.

How did my generation allow this to happen? We were anti-establishment, anti-war. We fought for civil rights and equal rights for women. We inhabited communes and lived off the land. We revered nature and peace and love for all. Yet, as the sixties and seventies turned to the eighties and nineties, we drifted into apathy. We turned our eyes to the 'American way' and quit seeing beyond that. It wasn't intentional. It was just a natural evolution. But the earth was counting on us. And I'm afraid we let her down.

I was an anti-war activist in college because I carried the generic fear of nuclear holocaust in my very cells. Seeing the old fall-out shelter signs in ancient school gyms still brings back the memories of preparing a fall-out shelter with my grandma, before the Cuban Missile Crisis was resolved. And the days of air-raid drills at school where we got under our desks to save us from nuclear attack! I slept with a radio in my bed headboard, turning it on if I woke up at night, just to make sure things were still ok.

I fear my grandkids will end up needing a similar assurance that the earth will live another day.

So we live with this grief. It ebbs and flows like other sorrow. Feel the feelings when they arise. Use the toolbox. And don't hide from it. Though we might feel powerless, there are things we can do. It might feel like a drip in a bucket, but focus on your corner of the world, your community, your neighborhood, your block. If we help change what we can see, feel, taste, and touch each day, the ripples can grow and become a movement. And maybe a brighter future.

PART IV: OTHER GRIEF CHALLENGES

This section addresses grief from different directions, from the perspective of your own loss and healing, universal difficult times, spiritual questions, and how to help others. There are times when grief tugs harder at our heart, and times when obstacles make the struggle more arduous. And as we move through this grief journey, we'll also pause and ponder our own life cycle.

Holiday grief

There are times when grief becomes more palpable. It finds its way to your belly, leaving a trail of visceral sadness. Holiday seasons are among those times. The heart softens, and the edges of loss feel sharper.

The path of your sadness depends on the history of holidays and your relationship with your loved one. Which holiday season had the most meaning in your family story? Where do your early memories lie? Were your holidays happy, or clouded by trauma? Think about your family celebrations of holidays, birthdays, anniversaries, Mother and Father's Days - how about any unique annual celebrations? Were summer holidays celebrated in a big way? Like so much else, this is a part of your grief story, helping you honor and come to a deeper understanding of why you grieve the way you do.

My family loved to celebrate holidays and birthdays. Every birthday, my grandparents made homemade ice cream. The birthday person got to pick the flavor. The endless cranking of the handle still holds a happy, tiring memory.

I loved Christmas. My grandparents owned a small-town grocery store/gas station, open seven days a week, twelve hours a day. Thanksgiving, Christmas, and Easter were the three days they closed - a loose term. Their home was connected to the business, and if someone called and said, "Fern, I ran out of milk. Could I pick some up quick?" the time would be taken to get that milk. But otherwise, we all were able to be together in the house, not in the little cubby kitchen off the store, the usual gathering place between customers.

Christmas dinner at Grandma's house was the peak of the busy Christmas season – the season where my happy memories and my sorrow meet each year. It's tucked into tinsel and twinkling lights that brightened the early evening darkness. It's in carols that accompanied the blustery wind. Friends gathered for shopping and fun, while families planned the holiday feast, nested in the warmth of tradition. Church events celebrated Christ's birth. Attending midnight Mass with my grandparents still holds a memory of awe and wonder, awakening my childhood heart even today. Winters were engraved with seasonal joy and laughter, a time when we were at our best. A time of gold and glitter.

That is until it wasn't. What happens when the season comes around and the glitter doesn't rub off? As much as Hallmark would have us think only happy holiday thoughts, there's human pain that bright lights and cheerful Santas won't erase. Where do we fit in a universe that seems so merry and full of celebration when we aren't?

My mother died in October. That holiday season I attended a gathering of three hundred people who carried grief, fresh grief, a first Christmas without a loved one grief. There were beautiful poinsettias, words of warmth, a sense of community, but not one single glimmer of glitter. This event was a holiday memorial service for people who had lost someone they love that year – people like me. There was a somber "reading of names." I swear when I heard Mom's name, I half expected to see her walk up on that stage and wave - and find a way to pull out pictures of her grandkids like she always did. My brain knew that wasn't going to happen, but my heart wanted her to answer the call.

This was the first holiday without. Without what, you might ask. Well, we really don't know until we get there. No one is prepared for the first holiday without a loved one. We don't know what to expect. As the season approaches, there's no way of telling what we'll miss, what will release the tears that burden our hearts so unceasingly. Will it be the mere emptiness of a chair? Or an absent walker? Maybe it'll be the lack of a certain caroler that gets us, or the lack of a traditional dish at the table. We prepare our hearts for the gaping holes, but it's the seeming "little things" that break us – the scent of perfume, the roughness of corduroy against a cheek, the taste of an anise cookie. Where would my memories of Mom land?

Having spent many holidays without my dad, my heart was used to his tugs as I took over the making of his traditional dish - cranberry fluff. I no longer saved up change for his family's annual Christmas day competition of penny ante poker. That tradition died with Dad.

His memories are now mixed with my wishes. I wish my kids knew him. I wish I could tell him he was an awesome dad. And I wonder each year - how can it be Christmas without Dad?

My Grandma's spectacular Christmas dinners are long since passed. I still see her bustling about, setting the perfect table still totally relaxed, using the good dishes, trying new recipes along with the regulars. There was always an extra person or two at her table. No one was allowed to be alone on Christmas. She was always the last one to sit down, apron still tied, cheeks flushed by oven heat. She molded my Christmases with her love and her spirit - and her baking. Every Christmas cookie I bake and deliver comes from her heart that beats in my soul. Each gift I make should have a label that says, "Made with love by Vicki and her Grandma Fern's spirit."

Our baby boy's stocking is hung each year. His Snow Baby angel is the last, most reverently hung ornament on the tree. On Christmas eve, the annual reading of The Littlest Angel takes place. The littlest angel is a little boy. He gives God a gift of his box of prize possessions, and God uses it to make the star of Bethlehem. And the wishful counting of years continues. He would be three, ten, fifteen, thirty…. He should be here. I think back to the Christmas before he was born, his stocking already hung with the others, and the stuffed duckie that Santa placed in it on Christmas morning. And I ask each year, silently to myself, how could the only thing left of my son be a Snow Baby ornament and a stuffed duck?

But the year of my mother's death I was vulnerable to new hurts. What would be the thing, the one tiny thing that would draw the first tears? Would it be the silent echo where Mom's laughter should be? Or the absence of those irritating jingle bell earrings she always wore? Or maybe it will just be the constant heaviness in my chest.

So, what can we do to prepare for what we feel totally unprepared for?

The first thing we do is honor our pain. Remember, if we hadn't loved someone deeply, we wouldn't feel so sad and lost. Stay connected to others. Be with people you love. Surround yourself with their comfort. Talk about your loved one. Share stories. Reminisce.

One of the first assignments my clients received, and now I share with you, is to find the balance between going on with life and taking time to grieve. Hold space daily for your loved one and thoughts of your holidays together. Set aside grief time – more at first, less as time goes on. Take that time to let the feelings wash over you. Cry, pray, yell – whatever there is to feel. Once the time is over, get up and tackle a challenge. This may be as big as a whole day of activity or as small a victory as taking a shower.

Make every effort to go to dinner, holiday concert, church service, the *Nutcracker*, or whatever feels available to you. Your first inclination will be to avoid the holiday entirely. But, let the presence of others lift you and carry you through. You might fear that you'll be a "downer" to others, and not want to ruin anyone else's holiday. I promise you that won't be the case. People who love you want to be there for you. Set realistic expectations for yourself, and don't try to act like you're fine. You're not. No one expects you to be.

Journal your feelings. It might be just notes, or it could become a letter to your loved one, telling them how much you are missing them.

Remember that we heal, but our life is changed in such a way that it'll never be the same again. What we do with that reality dictates our definition of healing. The holidays, the anniversaries, will get easier. There'll be joy, laughter, and love again, but no matter how many years go by, a song, a smell, a thought will bring back the memories, hitting us behind the knees and we briefly lose balance. My dad died nearly fifty years ago, but at Christmas the tree triggers feelings. He always had a small gift hidden in the branches for me the night of the church Christmas program. A vulnerable spot in my heart is hit, and tears rush to my eyes, validating he's still a part of me.

Remember your loved one's life, and your connection with them. Mitch Albom writes in *The Five People You Meet in Heaven*, "Lost love is still love…it takes a different form that's all. You can't see their smile or bring them food or tousle their hair or move them around a dance floor. But when those senses ease, another heightens. Memory. Memory becomes your partner. You nurture it. You hold it. You dance with it." [41]

For this holiday, purchase a memorial tree ornament. Wrap it up and tuck it in a special place after Christmas. Every year there'll be a soft moment, a pause to hold your memories. We added an angel for Mom in 2004. The tree tells the story of our family: children's ornaments, mementos of celebrations and friends, and memories of those no longer with us.

Always, and especially around the holidays, please take care of yourself. Get rest, eat good food, go for walks. Connect with others. Deal with feelings about your loss. Listen to soothing music. When laughter comes, allow it. There will still be plenty of tears.

As the years pass, you'll find ways to keep your loved one's memory alive during the holiday season. After getting through that first year of the unknown, someone might just get out a favorite recipe, like my dad's cranberry fluff, and you'll find it at the Christmas table. Every year thereafter, it will be a part of Christmas and you'll remember. Just as I smile remembering Dad as he mixed part of the recipe on Christmas Eve to "overnight the flavor", or how he thought it a personal affront if it didn't all get eaten. "The leftovers will separate and not be as good," he'd say. Someone always brought up the time he still had on one of Mom's aprons for a Christmas Eve picture – the one with the reindeer on it with the nose that lit up.

Christmas memories will warm us. The age-old debate that Mom and Dad had every year – how do you put the icicles on the tree – throw them in handfuls (Dad) or take three or four at a time, and neatly put them on each branch (Mom). That was never resolved. But memories like that tell a story of your holiday.

Keep a separate container for the special ornaments – the ones Gram brought back from trips to her beloved Colorado, the delicate antique Christmas bells from Great-grandma Ide. And Snow Babies and angels.

This Christmas, as we completed the decorating of the tree, that tender moment came when it was time for Matthew's Snow Baby angel. I opened the small box it was stored in. It was empty. Panic rose in my throat. It was like I lost him all over again. It took a whole day to find it. I give credit to the universe, as I felt guided to this round box with Christmas violins on it. It always sits on the coffee table among greens for the season, holding extra ornament hangers. I opened it and there was Matthew's Snow Baby angel wrapped in tissue paper as cozy as could be – like it was its home. I wept with relief.

I promise you'll get through the season, the first holidays, birthdays, anniversaries. There'll be tears. There'll be sadness. There'll be questions without answers. There'll be loneliness and sorrow. But there'll be love. The love that lives in your heart can't be erased by death. It's yours forever. We gather what is left behind as a legacy and hold it to our cheek like a warm blanket.

Ecclesiastes 3:1 is engraved on my parents' headstone. It reminds me whenever I visit "to everything there is a season, and time to every purpose under heaven."[42] Cherish the seasons of life that included your loved one. Like all of life, this is another part of the journey that will one day lead all of us home.

Complicated grief

Living through loss is difficult. It's hard. But there are certain situations that make it more challenging. If the grieving process is disrupted or interrupted, the journey becomes a longer and more complex road. This is complicated grief. It occurs when an event, relationship, or circumstance blocks us from going through all the stages and disrupts the natural progression of sorrow. We can get stuck in a certain stage. We can shut down the feelings and bury them deeply. We can torture ourselves with second guesses and unresolvable guilt and shame.

A loss that has complicating factors always benefits from seeking professional help.

Processing death in a natural disaster can lead to complicated grief. Feelings can be delayed as the shock and trauma, initially, tends to take over the brain's work. For example, if a massive tornado destroyed your town, leveling your home and killing your spouse, the numbness of trauma, the need to find shelter, clothing, food, water, basic survival needs would be forefront in your brain, with a muffled voice in your roaring ears crying, "My husband is gone." How and when you begin to process his loss depends on how quickly the survival needs are met – how quickly your brain moves beyond that shock and into the sorrow – a whole other trauma. As you begin to face his death, you'll also be processing that everything the two of you had is gone. Life is changed forever in so many ways. That is complicated grief.

There's complicated grief that results from feeling responsible for the death of a loved one. What if it was you who left something on the stairs that your loved one tripped over and fell to their death? What if you convinced yourself your friend's talk of suicide was just attention-seeking, before you got the call? What if you backed the car over your beloved family dog? What if your mother died in childbirth birthing you? What if your father died saving you from a fire? What if you told your son to walk home from his friend's because you didn't have time to pick him up, and he was run over and killed? These are all stories of inconsolable grief. Relentless grief. The overwhelming sense of guilt these horrors leave feels unsurvivable. They complicate your grief because you can't get to it. It remains buried in self-loathing and blame. It's stuck. It takes getting out from under the burden of guilt to get to the sorrow of your loss.

A complicated grief may occur when you have a fractured relationship with the person who dies. Years ago, there was a feud in my husband's family. This resulted in no contact with his mother or siblings for a year. His oldest brother, Stephen, was an artist, a creative soul with mental health issues who depended on his parents. He didn't drive, so even though he wasn't involved in the conflict, this fracture kept him away from us. The first interaction we had with my husband's family was a few months later – a Saturday morning call from his younger brother, telling us Stephen had been found dead – an apparent heart attack. The sadness of our children, the guilt of my husband, complicated his loss of Stephen – a big brother who took him on great adventures in their younger years, a source of happy memories. It was confusing for our children. Stephen was the quirky uncle who offered them coffee as toddlers, brought them massive hand-made cakes and outdated cereal and giant stuffed animals, who made them beautiful origami and hand-painted little boxes for their treasures. They never got to say good-bye. It took his death to bring the rest of the family together again. But talk of Steven always has a stumble, the tripping over his loss, the "we should have been there" left hanging.

My grandmother's sister quit speaking to her when she turned Catholic. The last words my Baptist aunt said were "You're going to hell." The rift lasted ten years. Fortunately, there was reconciliation before either became ill. But Grandma carried regret of wasted years when her sister died a few years later.

I went through similar stories with grieving clients – broken relationships, holding on to anger and pride. Some reconciled. Others not. Sometimes the fracture went on so long the original story became blurred. Everyone held on to their wounds, figuring the other would make the first move. Then someone died. No resolution, no reconciliation, no good-bye. Just the grudge, bitter and heavy.

There was a family of adult siblings that didn't speak for years – starting with a disagreement over their mother's nursing home placement. One of the siblings had a heart attack. She survived a week. This gave everyone a chance to reconcile, to say the words that needed to be said. The siblings, including my client, chose not to do this. Her death didn't offer a chance for healing either. She had made her wishes known – no funeral, no celebration of life, no grave side service. No family gathering to soften years of anger. No good to come from her death.

As a child, I experienced complicated grief in the death of my biological grandfather, my mother's dad. A raging alcoholic, he was a bad husband and father, heaping trauma on my mother's childhood. He and my grandma divorced early, but he continued to come around – the drill of turning over a new leaf of sobriety, turning to terror as he abused and betrayed. The last memory I have of him sober was a year before he died. He was welcomed into our home, yet again, forgiven and clean shaven. He went to meetings, looked for work, made amends. Then the morning cups of covert whiskey began, hidden first in coffee, then just straight up. The painful disappointment arrived. Mom was done. Grandma had been done for a long time. Dad kicked him out of the house. I was sad. Like many who fail their children, he tried periodically, to be a good grandpa. By my seven-year-old standards, he was. He brought me presents and told me stories of great adventure. He spared me his darkness. But there he went, disappearing from my life. Everyone else seemed relieved.

The next year, I received a gift in the mail – a Crayola crayon set with what seemed like a million colors, and a crayon sharpener. There was no card, but I knew it was from Grandpa. Soon after, Mom heard from an ex-wife in St. Louis that she had set him up in a rooming house and made sure he had food to eat. A few months later, the next call came. He was hospitalized with end stage cirrhosis of the liver. Mom went, forgiving him for the last time, and finding peace in that. He died days later. I vividly remember that trip to St.

Louis. Mary, his second or third ex, did a lovely job for a man who could've ended up in a pine box and an unidentified grave. I remember that the room in the funeral home was a misty haze of pink walls, chairs, curtains. I wore a white blouse and a knife-pleated blue skirt with suspenders. I recall the cool leather of the limousine seat on the back of my bare legs as we rode to the cemetery. I also remember the trip to his room in the rooming house after, where an opened closet door revealed floor to ceiling empty liquor bottles. I was the only one who cried for a man whose only positive legacy was that he was my part-time grandpa – a fairly good one, for what it was worth. There was never any reminiscing or memorializing, except in my little girl heart. The only talk of my grandpa was between me and my dolls.

Mom experienced a classic complicated grief when my father died. Sharing this family secret feels vulnerable, but it might bring comfort to any of you with a similar story. Your circumstances may be different, but the feelings – you'll recognize the feelings.

I've referred to my parents' marital troubles prior to Dad's death, and my role as the family counselor. There were several precipitating factors to their current issues, but the fatal one was becoming too close to a couple who were now their "best friends." My parents and the couple visited my husband and I in Florida. By the end of that visit, I warned my parents they were getting too close, and I felt uncomfortable around them. They assured me it was fine, but when we returned to Illinois, I learned differently. One afternoon my dad "dropped by" my townhouse to say hi. This devolved into a confession that he was having an affair with the wife of said couple. I took on my classic role. My advice, my edict, my command was it had to stop. If it didn't someone would get hurt. I didn't mean their feelings. I knew this situation presented mortal danger to one or more of the parties involved.

We never spoke of it again in the three months between the visit and his death. I let one perfect opportunity slip away. He and I did an early morning fishing date during a visit to their cabin on the Iroquois River. I treasured time with Dad. We didn't get out often just the two of us. The words were on my tongue, but I didn't want to spoil the moment. It was easier to tell myself that, of course, he'd listened to my counsel. One of my "if onlys" in my dad's death was what if I had asked him about it, allowed him the time to process his own feelings about this marital fracture. But I didn't.

I told him it had to stop. It didn't. When he died, letters and other evidence of the affair were removed from his work file cabinet, a pre-arranged "in case of my death" pact he had with a friend. Confirming this was through a strange, cryptic phone call - that the "job" was done. Of course, the "best friends" couple was there to comfort and support my mother.

Mom had guilt and regret about the night Dad died. Her last words to him were in anger, as was his response. She didn't try to stop him from leaving. She didn't call his dad to intercept him, an age-old pattern when all else failed. But she was able to navigate through the initial shock and trauma, be carried through the rituals of those first days. She would never have to know of the betrayal. Her memories could be only those of a loving and loved wife who made it through twenty-five years of marriage with all its ups and downs. The good memories would outweigh the bad.

But that wasn't to be. It seems the woman confessed to her husband the night after Dad's death. The man kept his secret for several weeks, then took it upon himself to share this information with my mother. She had a right to know, he said. She was just beginning to see life out from under the veil of shock. All the protection, the cleaning up after Dad, went down the drain. From that moment on, Dad became the enemy. He was the love of her life, from the first round on a Ferris wheel when she was sixteen. Now he was not only dead, he was dead to her. Her heart hardened to his memory. She closed off the torrents of grief that still waited to be released.

I'd like to tell you that this turned out well. I'd like to tell you that she was able to get help and process her rage and hurt. I'd like to tell you that she was able to continue to grieve and find a place for her good memories. But that wasn't the case. She eventually came out on the other side, but her grief remained buried under bitterness. In between there was a year of too much vodka, too much Valium and too much anger. There was a suicide attempt and a stay in a mental health unit. I grieved for my mom as I continued to heal from the loss of my father. He may have been human and vulnerable in his mid-life crisis, but all the good I've already told you about him remained true.

My mother was not meant to be alone. She had too much abandonment in her early life to suddenly become an independent woman who didn't need a partner. She met my stepdad at an

American Legion Bingo night. Despite him coming on the scene at the tail end of her self-destructive path, he stayed and waited. In my searches of my writing, I came across a note he sent Mom seven months before they were married. In it he quoted a verse from Ephesians and ended with "I pray this for you, Bonnie. Don't look for miracles, just accept His love with an open heart and mind."

She stopped drinking and taking pills. She started to take care of herself again. She married my step-dad – a good man who was a total opposite of my dad in many ways. Life went on. But no one was ever able to reminisce about my dad around Mom. There were no smiling remembrances of our life together, events I remembered and cherished. Her only memories were negative. His betrayal blocked the sunlight of their life before. Dad became my own private memory. No siblings to share with or Dad's family, who also became the enemy by association. I try to keep his memory alive based on the great guy he was, the cool dad, the best friend, the community leader. He was all these things as well as being lost in the shadows of a mid-life tragedy. It means so much to share memories with his old friends and my high school friends. Over the years, I've shared stories with my kids and grandkids. He would've been a good grandpa, the onery one who took them on adventures and let them stay up late. They would've loved him. You know, everybody loved Jimmy. I wish they'd been able to hear stories from their grandma about him to add to the depth of his memory. But they only heard negative from her. A complicated grief.

You might judge my choices. You might think I should've told my mother, or encouraged my dad to confess. I was a twenty-four-year-old only child; my family role was counselor/protector. It was what I did. As I matured and engaged in my own therapy, I extricated myself from that role and a new kind of relationship evolved for my mother and me - one she never quite understood. But back then, after my dad died, I knew what she could tolerate, what would destroy her. I never questioned whether it was a right or wrong decision. It was my function. A complicated grief.

A loss with complicating factors always benefits from professional help. Any trauma can lead to interference of a natural grief process. In these situations, a therapist can help you navigate your journey to the other side. Leaving yourself in the limbo of love and hate leads to serious disruptions of other relationships. If left untended, it can develop into a depression or physical illness. Even in the darkest, most complicated of circumstances, you can get to a point of healing.

If any of this awakens memories of complicated grief for you or your family, take time with your journal and honor those feelings.

When someone loved by a child dies

A child's first loss is the beginning of their grief story and tags along with every future loss. As the adults in our children's village, we impact how they'll deal with loss. We are their safe place and most trusted teachers. With our help, they can come to a budding understanding of the cycle of life and the impermanence of our time on earth, while acknowledging the mysteries of how it all works. Let them ask questions. Answer the ones you can. Don't be afraid to answer that you don't know. It's ok for them to understand that none of us are experts on death.

The one thing we know for sure is that we hurt when someone or something we love dies. Honoring this truth for your child is the greatest act of kindness and comfort you can offer.

If a person or pet lived a long life, and the child was able to say good-bye, it makes the circle of life feel more natural. While there's sadness and emotional pain, peace and acceptance comes. But what if it's a parent? Or a sibling? Or a friend? Or a classmate?

When my daughter was ten years old, she experienced multiple losses. On one weekend, her grandmother was in the ICU, her aunt died, and she got word that her beloved music teacher died after giving birth to her first child. While she loved and cared about her older relatives, it was her teacher's death that affected her most. Her teacher was young, talented, and adored. She was gifted in her work, igniting a love of music in her students. The year before she'd talked my sports focused son into being the Pigaloo Chief in *Treasure Island* so I knew she was a miracle worker. She was a special young lady. My daughter grieved by taking part in the community rituals honoring her teacher. Because she was a zebra in the last play with her teacher, we went to Build-A-Bear and created a stuffed zebra, with a heart tucked inside, for her newborn son who wouldn't know his mother. Within that next year my daughter's grandmother, two grandfathers, and the mothers of two classmates died. She was confronted with loss, but also with the reality that mothers die, and that gifted young women die. Nothing felt safe for some time. These early losses define her grief story. She grew into an empathetic adult with a very vulnerable heart. She now works as a pediatric hematology/oncology nurse, a sweet soul that doesn't hide from death.

Counseling is always helpful. But if there is multiple loss such as this or other trauma surrounding the loss, counseling is essential for your child and family. Little ones often process death more straightforward than adults. The walls of denial haven't been built yet. Euphemisms aren't a part of their vocabulary. Their sadness will be felt and expressed in many ways – tears, anger, physical symptoms, or in their behavior. Whatever form it takes, their feelings need validation and a safe space.

It's often our own challenges with death that complicate this process. Dealing with our own grief, our own mortality, and trying to protect our children from sadness, all contribute to our pulling them back from their sorrow. Rather, stay with them. Answer questions and acknowledge there are many answers none of us have.

I highly recommend several children's books. I mentioned *The Fall of Freddy the Leaf* in my grief story of Matthew. Leo Buscaglia dedicated this sweet book about the life of a leaf named Freddy "to all children, who have ever suffered a permanent loss, and to the grownups who could not find a way to explain it."[43] If asked, I would tell anyone that *Freddy* is the best book ever written about grief for children AND adults.

Tear Soup, by Pat Schwiebert and Chuck DeKlyen, was a favorite of my colleagues who worked with children. It's the story of Grandy, described as an "old and somewhat wise woman" who dealt with a great loss by making tear soup. "Because of her great loss, Grandy knew this time her recipe for tear soup would call for a big pot. With a big pot, she would have plenty of room for all the memories, all the misgivings, all the feelings and all the tears she needed to stew in the pot over time." [44] At the end of *Tear Soup* there are resources and notes about how to help a child through grief, as well as adults.

Other good children's books include *The Invisible String* by Patrice Karst. She weaves a lovely story of a very special string that connects people who love each other, even when they're apart. This string connects us in any situation, but also when one is in heaven.

Lifetimes: The Beautiful Way to Explain Death to Children, by Bryan Mellonie and Robert Ingpen, is a straightforward book about death and dying. It begins with "there is a beginning and an ending for everything that is alive. In between is living."[45] They go on to speak of the life cycle of plants, animals, and people.

These books will bring comfort but will also birth questions. Be prepared to listen and answer what you can. Help your child find a place for his loss. Give her the opportunity to remember, by talking, drawing, music. Help him to put together a memorial.

There are grief camps in most larger communities that provide respite for children who have experienced loss. These offer a sense of the normal, being in nature, with counselors and groups trained to help a child with sorrow.

There's a debate as to whether young children should be a part of the rituals of grief. Should they attend visitations, wakes, funerals, gravesides? Yes to all, with caveats. First, it depends on the child's age. If you have an infant or toddler, weigh the questions more for yourself than the child. What works best for you and your circumstances? If preschool or young school age, it's helpful for the child to be a part of these rituals of saying goodbye and honoring their loved one. If you know a visitation is going to be going on for an extended length of time, arrange for your child to take breaks, perhaps with a familiar sitter or an older cousin. With older children, there should be no question. Attendance is required. It may be difficult, but older children need to understand the value of gathering, of support, and the rituals of honoring who they've lost.

Answer any questions your child has before the events. Tell them what to expect, and what you expect of them. Examine your own feelings about them being in attendance. If you question whether you can manage your own grief and your child's, ask for help. It's important that your child be able to join the village that loved who they've loved and lost. They need to be given the opportunity to grieve with their tribe.

All that said, if a child is adamant that they refuse to attend, explore, and see if there can be a way to work this through. If not, don't turn it into a more traumatic event by power struggling. Use your judgement as the adult and make what feels like the best decision.

Answer any questions they might have afterwards. My grandchildren are now reaching the age of curiosity. Since I'm the senior member of the family, they ask me many questions. I try to answer them as simply and as truthfully as possible. It's not necessary to over-answer. Watch a child's eyes closely and observe their body language. You'll know when they've heard enough. Just the facts, ma'am. If we take a breath, we might hear more from them and their thoughts and feelings.

Helping others

Your grief story influences how you respond to another's loss. Prior to my dad's death, I had no idea how comforting and meaningful others' condolences could be. Being there, sending food and flowers and memorials, kind words – they all have meaning. If you have a complicated grief or trauma you're still processing, it may be difficult to be fully present for others. But there's always something you can do to comfort. A card with a thoughtful note and a shared memory can be a meaningful act of love.

Comfort. Be there. Sometimes the best gift you can offer is silence, or a simple "I'm so sorry." Just sitting beside a grieving person brings comfort. A hug, holding a hand, wiping tears – all mean more than we could ever imagine, often more than words.

But if you do offer words of comfort, be aware of things to avoid. Refrain from telling a hurting soul who has just lost a child or spouse that their loved one is in a better place, that it was God's will, or it's a part of God's plan. From personal and client experience, with few exceptions, no matter how much faith a person has, this is a time of struggle with God. My response to the God's plan cliché is that God is all powerful, and surely, he could've come up with a Plan B that would've saved my son. C.S. Lewis after the death of his wife, wrote "Don't come talking to me about the consolations of religion or I shall suspect that you don't understand."[46] You can believe, and hold on to faith, without agreeing with everything God does. If you're in the early phases of grief, it's likely you're having some hard conversations with Him.

A better place. What is that? Whatever it is, I still imagine my son would've preferred playing football with his brothers in the back yard on a crisp autumn afternoon, falling into crunchy leaves covering the touchdown line.

And never tell anyone that you know how they feel if you don't. If you haven't lost a child or spouse, or a sibling or a mother, don't presume to know anything about how the person is feeling. Even if you have, you can never know exactly how another is experiencing their loss.

But, if you've had a similar loss, do share sensitively. Women who shared their grief stories saved me when my son died. They offered concrete evidence that life could and would go on, when I thought it impossible. Then I paid it forward. For several years, after Matthew died, whenever I saw an obituary of a silent birth or infant death, I sent a card and note. I echoed to them what those who went before shared with me. It was also a factor in my practice. I wasn't just a therapist guiding them through the stages of grief. I was also a mother who had lost a child. Sharing your grief story with another, and listening to theirs, is the most valuable gift you can offer. Three months after my dad died, a high school friend lost both his father and mother in that short time. When I went to their visitations, we just hugged and stood there holding each other for a long time. He whispered tearfully "You know!" Yes. I did.

Don't be afraid to talk about your friend's loved one. You might be hesitant to bring up the name, fearing that you'll make them sadder, but it's comforting to know that others remember. Share with a grieving person your thoughts or memories about their loved one. In doing so, you're giving them a gift.

It's natural to say to someone who is hurting or sick, "Let me know if you need anything." It's a thoughtful thing to say. But don't expect that person to call and ask you to come over, or go the store for them, or take the kids for an afternoon, or do a load of laundry, or cook a meal. They will not call. They will not ask. Their entire pool of energy is focused on putting one foot in front of the other - getting through a day. The onus is on you. Call again. Tell them you're bringing dinner over. Ask them what time would be best to pick up their grocery list because you're going to the store. Plan a play date with the kids. Bring coffees over and sit at the kitchen table silently sharing.

In a *New York Times* guest essay, Julia Halpert wrote of the support she received after her son died. "One friend paid to have my home's gutters cleaned and windows washed. Our family's veterinarian refused to let us pay for her pet care services for a year. Another friend gave us keys to her lake house to use when we needed to get away. Each spring, we find a hanging plant on our porch from the parents of a friend of Garett's. As brutally hard as it's been to walk this new path without my son, these actions have provided a glimmer of positivity amid my despair."[47]

There's always a need, and there is always something you can do.

A few years ago, a tornado wiped out a third of a town near us. Spontaneous food kitchens and warehouses for donations materialized. There were immediate offers for lodging. Like hundreds of others, we joined meal chains for those we knew and brought food and supplies to those we didn't. We picked up laundry to be done. You don't realize that everything a person is left with is covered in dirt, mulch, and pulverized glass crystals. Whatever you do, do something. Don't wait for a call from your friend who barely has the energy to get out of bed and, maybe, on a good day, take a shower. Asking for help takes way too much energy. Be there.

And there isn't a statute of limitations as to when your friend no longer needs you. The real grieving, the learning to go on in life with a piece of you missing, doesn't really begin until the rituals are over. Everyone goes home. Life goes on. Your friend needs you then more than ever.

Be sensitive to what another has gone through. There was a boy named Michael my freshman year of college who, for a minute, was the love of my life. My dorm roommate also had a Michael. Hers was her only brother who died in Vietnam. I can't tell you exactly how my narcissistic eighteen-year-old self failed my roommate. Was it that I saw the five by seven photo of a young boy in combat gear sitting on her study desk and never asked about him? I honestly can't tell you if she told me this was a picture of her brother, or that it was a picture of her brother who died two years before in combat, or if the subject ever came up. Or was it even sadder, that she told me he'd died, and I either ignored her feelings, or blocked out the information? Whatever the answer was, I failed. Talk of my Michael was constant. She listened. She discreetly left the room during open-door coed hours on Sunday afternoons. She remained quiet when I put a huge orange poster board on our door that read, in bold brown lettering, "Happiness is Michael." I don't recall what lead to the breaking point, the "I can't take it anymore" moment. All I remember is the tears. Aching, primal, puddling tears. I held her as she sobbed. She cried, "I can't stand that you have your Michael, and my Michael is dead!" Her white-hot pain blazed into my heart, teaching me a lesson I'll never forget. Be sensitive to others. You never know what they've been through. Care enough to know someone. We had only met a couple months earlier. If I could hide my shame in that fact, I would. But I can't. I should've known, and I should've been more sensitive to the feelings of my roommate.

Be conscious of the reality that you often don't know what burden another human being carries. Smile at the checkout clerk who never smiles. Her sadness may be sourced in some loss unknown to her customers. Hold the door for the cranky old lady whose only surviving sister may have just died. Wave at the scowling, harried driver who may be caretaking his wife dying of cancer. Be open to the briefest opportunities for connection, for kindness – a smile, a wave, or holding a door. You don't know who you're going to bring a moment's comfort, whose burden you may momentarily lift, who will be your Jesus in beggar's clothes.

A gentleman posted on the "It's okay not to be okay" Facebook page about having to pick up bananas at the grocery store the day his father died. He was aware that no one knew what had just happened to him. It has helped him to be sensitive of others around him. "Most people are hanging by a thread and our simple kindness can be that thread. We need to remind ourselves just how hard the hidden stories around us might be, and to approach each person as a delicate, breakable, invaluable treasure – and to handle them with care."[48]

Follow through on loving thoughts. When you look back, it'll be the times you failed to be emotionally generous that'll bring tears to your eyes. The glare, the rude shoulder shrug, the flipped bird, the unkind muttering. You'll remember these. The calls not made, the time not spent, the times you were too busy to listen. Those too.

So be kind to the stranger, but also call your mom. Leave a note of appreciation for your roommate. Hug your friend. Tell the postman thanks for his hard work. Watch as the little girl next door shows you her puppy's trick for the fifth time.

Life is precious. Love is precious. Don't let those intended acts of kindness collect dust in the vault of good intentions, where they molder into regrets. Choose to be generous with your heart and your time. Keep your eyes open. Notice. Be a part of this lovely, messy, quirky, wise human tribe. It comes back around. You really do reap what you sow.

There'll be times you really don't have any idea that your words are stinging another's grief. Then all you can count on is they might tell you, and you can say you're sorry. A few months after my dad died, we got together with old friends who had moved from the area.

As we were driving to a restaurant our friend said, "So Vicki, How's your dad? I always enjoyed talking to him." It was one of those moments when that thin layer of healing was peeled away from my heart, the pain made new. Our friend had no idea that he had unwittingly brought the hurt back. I told him about the accident. He felt terrible, apologizing, and later sent flowers and a lovely note to my mother, and a sweet card to me.

But there are also times that thoughtless words just come out. When Matthew died, my well-meaning elderly neighbor told me that maybe if we had taken him early, he would've survived. A well-meaning statement, likely true. But it tore my heart with guilt. I was his mother. I should've known. Something was wrong and I missed it, and I let my baby die. She didn't know her words would take me down that rabbit hole, but she might have thought a bit before she spoke - to a mama who had buried her baby the week before. She also didn't know that an insensitive invitation to a baptism had come in the mail that morning. Neither the sender nor the neighbor ever knew that this was the day I called my therapist for an appointment. If we think before we speak and understand the vulnerable heart of the newly grieving, we can do better. Have a heart for others. And in those moments, when we do unintentionally hurt with words, apologize. Do what you can to make amends.

I don't want to leave you fearful of saying anything to a grieving friend. Most often, your words will be a great comfort. If you don't have the right words, "I'm so sorry. What can I do?" will work every time. Or no words at all. Just sit and hold a lost hand.

Where do we go?

Your answer to this question profoundly impacts how you deal with loss. Even among the religious, there are many ways of viewing God and what life after death looks like. Do you have a deep religious faith? Is your faith based on a doctrine of heaven or other after life reward? Do you believe that good people who live a moral life are welcomed into this reward? Do you believe that you must be saved to enter heaven or other afterlife paradise? Do you have faith you'll see your loved ones again? If you believe in God, do you see God as a loving deity or a vengeful force?

You may not have a faith in God or an afterlife. You may be an atheist or just not in the habit of thinking in religious or spiritual terms. You might believe that death is death. Ashes to ashes. There's no other side of the veil or a heaven or paradise. You'll likely deal with loss and grief differently than those who rest in Biblical assurances or promises of other faiths. No matter the theological or philosophical questions, faith offers another layer of comfort for grief.

I have a fair amount of experience in different Christian denominations. They've shaped my relationship with God. My opinions, voiced here, are forged from sixty plus years as a seeker with remnants of trust issues. Take from them what you will.

The ability to hold on to a belief and its promises is a gift. As strong as faith may be, it is faith. Its definition is belief in something we can't see. But there are those willing to die in the name of God's, or other deity's or prophet's, assurances.

As unique and personal as our religious beliefs are, there is a universal need to know, to be sure, to have the right answer. And should our right answer contain our entrance to heaven, even better.

I started out in a lukewarm Lutheran family with a very Catholic grandmother. I remember as a five-year-old, my grandmother asking her priest, who had stopped by the store, if she should make sure I got to Sunday School more often. The priest, an old paunchy guy with a kind face and an Irish brogue, knelt to my level and asked me, "Young lady, do you love Jesus?" I said sure. He stood up and smiled at me and told my grandma that I was just fine.

I later converted to Catholicism. My first husband was Catholic and Grandma had paved the way. I never tired of the worshipfulness or mystery of the Mass, but twenty years later, following a move from our home parish, we attended the funeral of an elderly neighbor who was Mennonite. We found a unique sense of family in that little country church where he grew up. There were elderly members who remember coming to Sunday service in horse and buggies on their mothers' laps and all the generations that followed. We entered the world of getting "saved" to reserve our place in heaven. I got saved and baptized and renewed my commitment many times over the years. It was a lovely time of potlucks, coffees, wiener roasts and hayrack rides, caroling, and Bible studies. The pastor was the sort of man whose life reflected the light of Jesus. I loved that church, but I never fully embraced the concept that a certain prayer opened the gates of heaven to me, while those gates remained closed to my selfless servant Jewish neighbor and my saintly Catholic grandma, and every Muslim or Buddhist that I knew.

The politics of most churches often leads to disillusionment. Sadly, in a small church of multigenerational families, it caused discord that eventually closed the church. It was during that time that our son and his future wife became involved with a campus ministry at the University of New Mexico. We attended the denomination's local church when the kids were home for a visit. If our old church was like a small tight-knit family, this one was like a big, boisterous commune of people from every walk of life. We began attending regularly, appreciating the pastor, and embracing the many activities that this big diverse family engaged in – yes potlucks and gatherings and Bible studies and card nights and game nights – family. We loved these folks. Our then teen daughter got involved in the choir and shared her beautiful voice.

Now, I had Lutheran infant baptism, Catholic adult baptism, and Mennonite immersion baptism. So, I figured I was set. But it turned out you had to be baptized by immersion in this church after you embraced a specific set of Bible verses.

I might sound a bit cynical. I honestly don't mean to. I want to be respectful of all these faith experiences. But I was never one for embracing doctrine. I went along with it because I loved all the people and the presence of God in the gathering of family, of village. I always wondered, as a Catholic, what it would be like to really worship Mary, or feel God's grace touch me when I said those saving words as a Mennonite. But I accepted that I was missing some things and embraced what did bring me joy in the church, finding God in the message and Jesus in the people.

With this new church, though, I put on the brakes. I held off getting baptized because I wanted to truly find the sureness this time. I told the two ladies who were my mentors, that I compared it to faking an orgasm. (We got a laugh out of that!) You could go through all the emotions and reap some benefits, and make another happy, but you were left wanting. I didn't want it to be that way this time as it had been my whole religious life. But I eventually gave in because I finally accepted it was never going to happen for me. So, envious of all those glowing faces filled with the assurance of paradise, I got in the tub and pleased the masses. Having known what a real orgasm felt like, I knew, from a religious perspective, I was missing something deeply spiritual and fulfilling that others seemed able to attain. We went on in this church for a few years, until we were told that our daughter could no longer sing in the choir because she was dating a very nice young man who wasn't a church member. That immediately felt dysfunctional - way too restrictive and authoritarian – not my family. I couldn't assimilate that amount of exclusivity into my brain. We had to leave. I haven't been a regular church attender since.

I consider myself a thinking person. I try to figure things out. I like puzzles and mysteries. This is a trait I'm happy with, but also understand it can also act as a protection, a boundary. You know the game where you fall back confident that your partner will catch you? I'm not very good at that. Really, I'm not good at complete trust of anyone or anything – even God. I've accepted my reality. I cherish the few humans in my life that I would trust to fall into. But I don't have the innate capacity for the trust required to feel assured of heaven. I vacillate between envying and resenting those of you who do. In times of grief there is much comfort in a church, in the family of believers who surround you, in the words from the pulpit. It brings tears to my eyes as I write this and remember the love that has surrounded me in times of loss, aware that I now lack that unique community. I know my friends, neighbors, and family members – the tribe I happily dwell in will surround me and carry me, but there's a certain something about a church family. There's a peace that, yes, passes all understanding that carries you through. One thing for me, knowing the remnants of my own trust issues, is a church family can't abandon me. They're forced by commitment to love me like Jesus.

Over the years, I've embarked on my own spiritual journey, finding a solid relationship with God on His and my terms. I've embraced my unsureness. I think Jesus understands. I feel comfortable that I'll have answers when it's time for me to have those answers. But I've found a personal peace and spiritual connection I never found in a church's doctrine – except maybe watching my grandma's glistening eyes as the wafer touched her tongue.

Even if I can't trust the promise of heaven because of some missing piece in me, I do believe that there is something on the other side of the veil. I just don't know what that's going to look like. I know that no one else really knows either, but they have faith that they know. Somehow that's enough for them.

If there is a heaven or another side of the veil, I hope it's like

Randy Alcorn's description in his novel *Deadline*. One of his characters dies and enters heaven. The description of him leaving his body, and the welcome at the portal of heaven is very similar to our first birth, but now on to the next plane. Loved ones eagerly await and welcome you with joy. But it's the portal that gets me. Not only are you reborn to the next life, but you can also observe earth through this portal and intervene and intercede for your loved ones on earth.[49] Later, Alcorn went on to write a non-fiction book about heaven. It was lovely and filled with evidence that heaven exists. But, for me, the description in the novel, holds me suspended in wonder. This is what I hope is on the other side.

I recently spoke with a friend who has similar spiritual experiences to mine. She recounts a memory when a family member died too young. Her sister-in-law, a woman of deep faith, told her that she was comforted by the absolute confidence that their relative was with Jesus. My friend had tears in her eyes as she spoke of her sorrow that she lacked that faith and the comfort that comes with it. I cried for her because I understood.

I might not have that assurance, but I've heard too many stories of spiritual revelations and visits not to believe that there's something going on "out there." There are too many near death experiences of those who were clinically dead and brought back by medical intervention. I know there is research and theories that say it's hallucination and that, really, we're just gone. Or that it's what we want so it's the last thing we experience. But I don't buy it. There is just too much evidence of spiritual revelations and connection.

I have a dear friend who is in my small trust circle. She survived a near death experience. She is a strong, practical woman, not prone to exaggeration or wishful thinking. Her heart stopped during an acute illness while in the hospital. During her code, while the docs and nurses worked to revive her, she rose above her body, looking down on them, watching it all. She can quote verified words she heard. At one point she felt herself rising toward a white light. An indescribable calm and peace enveloped her. She felt surrounded by love and joy bathed in that light. She wanted to keep going, to enter the light, but a voice told her she was not ready yet, that she had to go back and complete her work. With that she descended back to her body and woke up intact shortly after. She recounted this to me with tears in her eyes, her voice hushed with awe. The last thing she said is that she no longer has any fear of death and will be ready when that time comes. Because she knows.

A musician friend spoke of a near death experience after surgery as nothing short of wonderful. There are also accounts of longer visits to the light by patients who met loved ones before returning to their earthly bodies.

In her book *Dying to be Me*, Anita Moorjani speaks of her near-death experience. "What I can only describe as superb and glorious unconditional love surrounded me, wrapping me tight as I continued to let go…Love, joy, ecstasy poured into me, through me, and engulfed me. I was swallowed up and enveloped in more love than I ever knew existed. I felt freer and more alive than I ever had." [50]

Before researching *Surviving Grief,* I didn't know how much literature there is to support near-death experiences. The events throughout all reports, case studies, and research are eerily similar. Some stop at the light, told to return. Others meet loved ones. Some recount events they couldn't have known but from a deceased relative. Some return with knowledge about their future. Others develop a degree of clairvoyance. But they all start with the leaving of the body, following the light and being told to return. The most universal commonality of all is the indescribable feeling of love, peace, and joy, and the absence of fear of death in the future.

Kenneth Ring, in his book on near death experiences *Heading Toward Omega,* finds that "one of the themes that runs repeatedly through the testimony of NDErs is that, though they believe in God and may continue to attend church, they are apt to describe themselves as spiritual rather than religious."[51]

As she encountered patients with near death experiences, Elizabeth Kubler-Ross deepened her own spiritual journey. In her memoir *The Wheel of Life,* she speaks of death as the experience of the butterfly, viewing death as the release of the butterfly from the cocoon of earthly life. "We are allowed to shed our body, which imprisons our soul the way a cocoon encloses the future butterfly." We're then "free as a beautiful butterfly returning home to God."[52]

In *Heading Toward Omega*, Ring reports case study findings that NDErs "were more likely to be more open to the concept of reincarnation than they had been before."[53]

Psychiatrist, Brian L. Weiss, wrote of near-death experiences in his book, *Many Lives, Many Masters*, in which he recounts therapy sessions with a young woman who regresses to past reincarnations during hypnotherapy, reliving many near death and death experiences.[54]

These authors are professionals who explored these subjects through the lens of clinical research and case studies. Their work has withstood the test of time. The patient reports are of a personal nature, but consistent enough in their accounts to lend their experiences credibility. What it finally comes down to is we won't really know until we know. And we won't know until it's our time. When we're allowed to see, to feel for ourselves, it'll all become clear. And I'm guessing it's going to be lovely.

PART V: THE TOOLBOX AND OTHER TREASURES

In this final section we continue our journey by exploring practical tools to get through it. First there's navigating a minute, then a day, then on to healing steps. From there we move on to find the means to remember our loved ones, allowing them to remain a part of our life – only in a new way.

In her poem "You May Be Gone", Donna Ashworth speaks to this.

> *You may be gone but I feel you when the cool breeze brushes past.*
> *You may be gone but I hear you when the music plays its last…*
> *You may be gone but your laughter is still my favorite sound.*
> *You may be gone but my darling you're ever all around."*
> *Always there. Just in different ways.*[55]

This chapter includes practical tools and information to assist you as you begin to imagine another future, so different than the one of your dreams. Some of these tools and ideas will seem alien. Just be where you are. Do what is available to you. This book is there for you wherever you are in your grief. What works for you now might feel worn out later, and something new will be worth a try. Keep it in a special door with your journal and timeline. Use it till it's dog-eared and worn.

Just as grief is universal, yet unique, so is getting through to the other side. There'll still be life to live, meaning to find, and joy to experience. There'll be precious days to discover, new things to learn, and people to love.

In the early days, we wonder about this idea of going on. It seems impossible to imagine. If we're fortunate, there are those left behind who need us. I say fortunate because they get us through the days that feel unsurvivable. It's a grinding, one step in front of the other, process to meet the obligations of what and who remains. It will feel like you lack the psychic energy to be there for your small children or your dead husband's elderly mother, but it'll come because we do what we must do. It leaves you wrung out, falling into dreamless sleeps, but you'll do it. Eventually, you'll look back with gratitude for those you couldn't leave.

The hours, days, and months of grief march on. Little by little we see light. How you get to the light is a journey no one can take for you. It's the final entry of your grief story.

The tools, suggestions, information, and words of comfort I offer are given to facilitate your journey – to provide you with a sense of control and purpose as you move through seemingly endless days. We start to find places to hold what can't be fixed.

I offer these next chapters as a menu of sorts, based on what's been helpful to my clients, my friends and family, and myself. Create your toolbox for healing from this menu. You'll also likely develop many of your own tools over time. I'd love to hear of them, as they might also help others one day.

Basic self-care

Breathe.

In an early chapter, we talked about the value of the breath, not just to stay alive but as a powerful tool for centering, anchoring, and holding. It provides a degree of control when it doesn't feel like any exists.

Pranayama is a yogic practice of breath regulation. In Sanskrit, "Prana" means life energy and "Yama" means control. It offers us the use of rhythmic abdominal breath as a vehicle for self-calming. Research shows that breath work is valuable to manage the anxiety and depression that comes with grief. This is true in the acute trauma period and as you incorporate self-care into your healing process. Physiologically, going to your breath relaxes muscles, stabilizes blood pressure, and increases energy. In the early days, maintaining this equilibrium is invaluable. So, take time each day to focus on your in/out abdominal breathing. You can be in a meeting, driving a car, at lunch with a friend. If you begin to feel tension or anxiety, start counting your breaths – in two three four, out two three four – and sense your abdomen as it creates the rhythm of your breath and the calming of your body.

Lean in, lean on

Our society tends to value independence and individuality. We like to view ourselves as rugged trailblazers, taking care of number one. That's fine for some cowboys, but it's bad for those of us who choose to be a part of a human community. There's an emotional regression that occurs in the early days of loss. Symbolically, we're birthed to a strange and alien world by the labor pains of loss. We return to the lower levels of Maslow's pyramid of needs. We seek survival, safety, love. We yearn to be carried and fed and put to bed. We need to be nurtured, nested, tended. This might conflict with a higher-level desire to be strong. But you will feel weak because you are weak in the dawning hours and days. You are broken, fragile, vulnerable. Let others surround you, hold you, lift you. Feel their hearts breaking for you. Eat their food. Let them fill your space with their love. The alone days will come, but not at first. Be brave enough to be in your fragility. Be courageous enough to be cast open to a primal need for your people.

Talk

Talk about your loss. Verbally process your grief. Your brain has had an emotional and traumatic injury. It throws all the data of this trauma onto a loop of thought - over and over and over – trying to make sense of what makes no sense. Because of this, you'll have a need to tell your story over and over and over. It'll like a compulsion. It's present in most loss, but if you've experienced a tragic unexpected loss, the shock is greater, and the loop lasts longer. Talk. Talk. Talk. If your tragic loss was part of a disaster, you may experience this later as the survival need for food, shelter, and sustenance kicks in first.

During the early days we tend to idealize who has died. No one is perfect, but for a brief time your loved one is. Best friends who heard every daily complaint about your spouse, will now hear that your deceased partner was a saint. Every good thing will flood your brain and come out of your mouth. And it will all be true. It's just that the daily mundane irritations and sources of spousal arguments aren't presently relevant. Your father-in-law may have sometimes been a bane to your existence, but right after his death, you'll only see him at his grandkids' ball games or carving the holiday turkey. It's a good thing. It's not lies, it's not denial. It's focus. The daily grit of life can turn us away from the good in those we love. It's only that ice water in the face, the shock that they're gone, that takes the mind's eye on a one eighty turn to the positive. Tell the stories that come. Smile through your tears as you remember those perfect moments that are now gone.

Get outside

Get outside every day, even if for five minutes. Stand on your porch. Have someone move a chair out there if needed. No matter how hot or cold or rainy it is – just be out there. Breathe in the air, let the breeze touch your hair. Listen – to trees, to birds, to life. Let nature nurture you. Honor your primal needs for grounded feet and felt wind. Being outside levels us, feeds us, reminds us life will go on even when we're not sure we want it to. It reminds us of our place in the universe. It offers light's energy and nature's peace.

Eat, sleep, move and wash

Now, back to those survival skills. This is the process of allowing the involuntary acts of habit to continue uninterrupted. We're talking the basic mechanics of swallowing food, closing our eyes, and placing feet one in front of the other. Food goes in your mouth. Chew it and swallow. You're handed a toothbrush with toothpaste on it. You automatically brush your teeth. You go to the bathroom. You go to your bed and lay down on your pillow. You close your eyes. You sleep. When you move, you step with a stiff gait, feeling awkward and unsure that this is the right way to do it. It is. You might think - that will never happen to me. But when someone you love dies it will. It won't last long but in the early hours of shock it's all you know.

In those hours, let others lead you, tend to you. Follow their instructions.

Move purposefully

If you're able to get exercise from the beginning, that's helpful.

But that may not be the case. Your first days might be spent barely mustering the strength to sit in a chair and hold your head up to look out the window. That's okay. You'll know when it's time to push yourself.

When that time comes, put on your shoes, and go for a walk. You might start out with no energy and dead weight legs, but if you keep going for ten minutes, the benefits will start to take over. Your legs will lighten, and your focus will sharpen.

A memory I hold is when my grandma died. We stayed at a motel in my hometown across the street from what had been my grandparents store/gas station/home. At dawn, I put on my shoes, crept over sleeping husband and children, and headed out. I'd never run, as an adult, in my little town, so it was a new perspective. I started out peeping in the windows of the store, jogging around back where the garden had been, and the bench where I shucked peas and ate strawberries. From there I hoofed it through the whole town — all the memories of childhood swelling in my heart, remembering a life cushioned by my grandma. That run gave me strength to get through a hard day.

Attitude

When muddling your way through grief's early stage of shock and fog, it's hard to muster a positive attitude. But you'll get to a place where you'll have a choice of where to focus. You'll start each day with that choice. Even in the worst of times, you can hear a singing bird, or smell dusty spring rain. There is no bad so bad that it removes all good. Your grief causes that shadowy veil, but some good will remain in the haze that surrounds you. Remind yourself every morning that you have a choice. At first, each day will begin with the smack of reality that your person has died, reminding you of your aloneness, taking with it all the light and all the birdsong. But as time goes on, each morning, there on the edge of wakefulness you'll start to decide to give this day a chance. One of your most useful tools will be choosing the direction of your daily focus. Beauty can always be found, no matter what the circumstance. Never miss the tiniest tease of it. In Ann Frank's diary, she wrote, "I don't think of all the misery but of the beauty that still remains."[56] We ultimately determine how life events impact us. We can't keep bad things from happening, but we can control how they define us.

Radical self-care: spiritual body work

This includes yoga, meditation, grief rituals, or any other practice you do that connects you more to the universe, God, the earth, and others on similar spiritual journeys. Since the pandemic eased, I've found a renewed connection to this spiritual life. Try things you've never tried. Through my research, I've engaged in new practices and rituals that have been healing. I tried ecstatic dance and sound baths. I'm a bit too tightly held together to truly appreciate ecstatic dance, yet for others it's a lovely meditative activity. But sound baths are a keeper. I plan to continue to take part in this beautiful meditative practice that uses sound bowls and soft gongs for a long time. I encourage you to explore. If you are already engaged in a practice, please return to it as soon as you can.

I also attended grief rituals lead by a death doula. A death doula (also known as transition doula, grief doula, or death midwife) is a person who helps the dying and their families through this life transition. Like a birth doula who assists in birthing babies to this world, a death doula assists in passing on to the next. These gatherings were profoundly moving and held space for those attending to express their grief in a safe place. The evenings ended with the creation of an altar of flowers, candles, and shared memories of those we mourned, symbolically returned to the earth through fire and water. Those attending the grief rituals were at all different stages of their grief. I recommend trying a grief ritual. The ones I attended were at a local yoga community, but you can also search grief doulas and contact for events scheduled near you.

I've practiced yoga for years, but because of COVID haven't been in a group practice for some time. Yoga is physically, spiritually, and emotionally restorative and healing. You can do it anywhere. My practice has included streamed classes from my former yoga community to Yoga with Adrianne on YouTube. She has a Yoga for Grief session available on her menu which is a gentle, restorative class. Do it where you can. But when you're able, get involved with a yoga community. There is support and healing there.

Incorporate meditation into your healing path. This can be guided meditations, meditation with a set intention for focus, or a more transcendental form of practice. Find what best works for you. There's healing and restoration for the spiritual and physical body in this practice. I do best with a more transcendental form where I sit quietly with a mantra leading me to a meditative state. And I recommend the sound bath meditation - my newest path to peace and energy.

Others may recommend Chakra healing, Reiki healing, Acupuncture as tools to try. Be open to whatever helps you to heal.

Journal

If you already had a commitment to journaling, that's good news. If not, I hope you've been able to use my prompts to get started. It'll become a natural practice like eating, sleeping, and moving. If you haven't already, please begin when you're able. It doesn't need to be a daily chronicling of your pain, though it can become one of your most healing routines. At first, use single words to respond to the prompts – whatever you're capable of. When my son died, it was six weeks before I really started to write. Once started, I didn't stop for six months. Now I had a place to put my sorrow.

Writing helps us discover what we feel. The act of putting a pen to paper becomes a path to healing. You never know what feelings will show themselves. It's like cream that rises to the top of raw milk. You wait for it to gather, then skim it off and make something good out of it.

Journaling is also helpful if you're stuffed with feelings you've kept held tightly inside. It's cathartic. It purges. It's like hitting a punching bag for twenty minutes or running five miles. Instead of pounding your grief into the pavement, you fling it onto the paper.

The following are some journaling ideas. One may become your best ritual of the day, while some will seem senseless to you. Take what works and leave the rest.

The journal letter

You may be left with the bitter taste of words – words you wish you would've said, words you wish you wouldn't have said. There might be another person involved in your loss that you have feelings to work through. The words are left with nowhere to go.

The journal letter can help you find peace. This is especially true if you have a complicated grief. Finding a place to put these feelings helps to bring some resolution over events that feel unresolvable.

Whether it's unexpressed anger and hurt, apology or forgiveness, the journal letter gets it out. These letters are for you, not anyone else. Sit down and write every word from your gut. Make it brutal in its honesty.

When you feel like you've said all you have to say and you're drained of feeling, a sense of peace will emerge. Honor your words. Have a ceremony, a rite of passage, and let go the burden. Get a fire-safe dish or go outside to the sidewalk. Light the edge of the paper with the flame of a candle. Lay it down and watch it burn. When it simmers to ash, it's a thing of the past, no longer able to weigh on your soul. It has returned to the earth.

I recently heard of another journal letter. Anderson Cooper's podcast about grief, "All There Is," had a caller who said she wrote a letter to herself from her estranged parent who died. In the letter she told herself all the words she yearned to hear from her parent. She told herself she was loved and cherished and was asked for forgiveness from her parent who had been absent and damaging in her life. She described this letter as the most healing act she had ever encountered.[57] I highly recommend this entire podcast. It's beautiful and poignant as Mr. Cooper reflects on his personal losses and speaks to other grief survivors.

Journaling for discovery

Sometimes we know there are feelings to get out, conflicts to resolve, but we aren't sure what they are. We sit with tears or anger right on the edge of consciousness, but we can't quite grab hold. Journaling can help you figure out what you're feeling. Emotions have been triggered by something – a word, a song, a smell.

Start by writing the events of the last twenty-four hours. First, it's like newspaper reporting, but soon it connects to feelings. Journaling becomes the pen and paper equivalent of retracing your steps searching for lost keys. Just as you find the keys in the couch cushion or under a stack of mail, you'll find the beginning of your mood tucked inside a coworker's frown, Nirvana on Spotify, the food truck you passed, or the foreboding shadow of the afternoon sun. Once you understand the trigger, you can work your way back to peace.

Gratitude journaling

There will be days, perhaps weeks, where you don't see one good thing to be thankful for. There's blackness all around. But there's always light, always something for which to be grateful. Even if it's the fact that you made it through another hour or one more day, or that you brushed your teeth, or that you got out of bed. Maybe it's the sunrise that tells you you made it through another night. Or that you breathe. Or that your neighbor hasn't missed a day of dropping by.

As you purposefully search for bright spots, they become easier to see. It's an exercise in mindfulness, a means of returning your heart to the good. It reminds you no matter how profound your pain, blessings and beauty are still present.

Dream journals

Years ago, my mentor told me that the heart of therapeutic material is in early memories and recent dreams. This also applies to grief. Your dreams play a role in healing. As the brain attempts to work through the trauma of loss, you'll likely find your dreams called into action – another level of consciousness on duty for the team. Even later a dream can pop up. You don't know why at the time, but it might become clear later. I'm waiting for clarity after a dream about my mother a few nights ago. In the dream, she had died, and we were picking out flowers. Someone was selecting pinks and reds. I started to cry and told them not those colors. Mom never wore pink or red because of her red hair. I saw it as a remnant of protecting my mother again. This time it was from clashing flowers.

There might be dreams of events from your past or symbolic dreams of fears and insecurities. You might dream you left your loved one somewhere unsafe or forgot them at a party. At first you might be frightened by these and be reluctant to examine them. Stay with them, though. They're crumbs left on the path to help you find your way through the pain.

Some dreams won't make sense at first, taking bizarre twists and turns. Some may become clear while others remain confusing somnolent wanderings. Others will smack you in the face with revelation and "aha" moments.

If your first waking feeling is sorrow or anger, there is a dream connected to those emotions. Follow those crumbs back to the night's dreamscape. Some mornings you'll wake up feeling like your loved one is still alive, and then be hit with that crushing reality that this isn't true. Your dreams gave you hope, only to crash into your sorrow again.

Keep a notepad at your bedside. If you wake in the night from a dream, jot down enough to assure you'll remember the content the next morning. Some will find use, while others remain jotted notes that will never make sense.

Art journaling

If you like to draw, this type of journaling could be a priority in your toolbox. As with other forms of journaling, you'll discover what there is to find. This journal may become sketches of lovely memories that take a clearer shape through your art. Or it may become a place for all the dark foreboding images of your fear and pain. Likely, a mix of both. Honor each one. Don't shy away from negative or dark sketches. There is something to be learned there. We often gain more wisdom from the darkness we travel through than the light.

Grief appointments

Grief appointments, which I briefly addressed in the Holiday Grief section, aren't, technically, journaling, but the process includes writing. Initially, loss is all encompassing. To focus elsewhere feels impossible. Everything you do is clouded by a haze of ongoing sorrow. If you find yourself laughing, it feels so foreign you fear it could become hysterical tears.

As time passes, you'll start to sense movement. You take the first tentative steps with your person tucked in your heart. Life calls. It pulls you back in. You must get your kids to school, return to work, call the plumber for the running toilet.

This first movement seems awkward and bumbling because it is. There're no written instructions to guide you through the coming months, and years.

This is when it's time for grief appointments. These are like worry appointments, a task in *Happiness Calling.* You'll need a notebook or paper and pen, a timer, Kleenex, and a boxful of memories. In the box, place pictures and mementos. This is your grief primer. Don't hesitate to put anything that will trigger you – ticket stubs, dried flowers, cologne, hair ties, beard oil, bath soap, a favorite sweater, music, videos, a voice mail. This sounds overwhelming, but it is the number one secret weapon to begin your journey back. It helps you to gain control over your sorrow. It won't make you grief free. But you'll be able to manage your sorrow and keep it from impinging on your ability to move forward.

At first, it's best to start with twice a day for thirty minutes. Don't go beyond that limit. You have a day to do. Over time, you'll be able to decrease to once-a-day. Then you'll find you need less time. Finally, you'll discover you don't need it anymore. The memory box will be put away in a place of honor. But for now, create a designated space as your grief spot. Sit down with your box, paper, pen, and Kleenex. Set your timer. And go. Dive into your memories. Touch, smell, see, taste, hear what you miss. Cry, yell, swear, plead, rage. Bang your fist on the table. The thoughts and feelings that come are important. Write them down. This isn't your journal, but you might discover topics you want to write about later. There are no rules to these appointments, other than don't hurt yourself, and stop when the timer goes off. At that time, put the box away along with your notes. Blow your nose and dry your eyes. Say, I'll see you later babe. And get up. You likely think it'll be difficult to stop and put it away, but the very act of doing so gives you an element of control. By allotting time for your sorrow, you continue to honor your loved one, but begin the arduous process of taking your life in a forward motion. When you get up from your grief appointment, do something – a walk, a phone call, a planned outing. Take a shower, plan a meal, style your hair. You aren't allowed to sit on the couch and continue your sadness. You now have a time for that, a place to put it. At first, it'll seem impossible. But, like everything, practice helps.

The rest of the day, if something triggers sadness, jot it down in your book to be dealt with at your next grief appointment. In doing so, you honor your grief and the validity of your feelings, but you take control. This is a simple exercise, but if you're faithful, it'll be extremely effective. Your day won't be burdened with chronic grief. It will be waiting for you at grief time.

Try to find a journaling tool that's right for you. You can mix n' match. You might be thinking that journaling sounds helpful, but what if you died and all this cathartic, cleansing writing was discovered? What about all those angry words you wrote to your loved one for leaving you like he did? Or what of that raging at your husband for not being more emotionally supportive of your grief. Or your bitterness toward your uncle who didn't attend his brother's funeral? Just because you felt it, you might not want everyone to know it. That's fine. These are your feelings, your private business.

I have many lovely journals with words about love, loss, anger, forgiveness. But I also learned to be prepared during a good journal session. Have a packet of loose-leaf paper or a roll of paper towels close at hand. When the emotion on the page gets rawer than the legacy you wish to leave, smoothly transition to the extra paper. You don't have to miss a beat. Suddenly, you're unedited. You get to use all the swear words your kids don't know you know. You can call names and fantasize about what you want to do to your uncle or spouse, or the person you grieve. When you get it all out, call in the burn pile or shredder. It's served its purpose. It's disposable. This editing tool can be used in any of the journal techniques to keep portions of your rage and pain private. If you discover something worth preserving during these therapeutic rants (and you likely will), jot down a phrase in your journal that helps you remember.

Managing symptoms: anxiety

When you experience a major loss, it's common to feel anxious or experience panic attacks. You're broken, vulnerable, laid bare. Anxiety is the brain's response to a nameless fear. Even after the initial shock, it's natural to feel anxious. It can range from mild restlessness and edginess to full blown panic. In the case of severe anxiety or panic, you're bombarded with multiple physical symptoms, such as racing heart, tightness in the chest, tingling, difficulty swallowing, sweating. It's accompanied by a dark feeling often described as a sense of impending doom. The first time you experience this level of anxiety it feels like you're dying. You fear for your life - afraid you're having a heart attack and losing your mind all at once. What's happening to your body is a normal physiological response to fear and danger. The chemicals coursing through your veins are for survival, a flight or fight response. This physical reaction prepares us to survive if we need to run very fast, climb a tree, or lift a car. The problem comes when your brain gets a wrong signal and starts screaming "Danger! Danger! Danger!" when there's no car to lift. The flight or fight system is activated. The amygdala starts things running amuck and misfires. But without an immediate physical threat in need of a superhuman response, you're suddenly stuck with an intense energy surge. It courses through your veins, creating all the symptoms that make up a panic attack. It feels like doom, chest crushing doom – until the chemicals dissipate. Then the feelings go away.

Sometimes there is a specific trigger. Other times not. With grief, all the overwhelming feelings you're confronted with are anxiety producing. A resulting panic attack could be linked to underlying fears that you aren't aware of yet.

It's important to remember that panic attacks are self-limiting, and no one ever died from one. It's just the getting through to the other side. One helpful tool, during severe anxiety is to ground yourself to the tangible things around you. Breath skills are helpful. Breath focus slows stress signals but is also a good grounding tool. And use your five senses. Touch the arm of a chair. Feel the texture of the fabric. Listen to birds sing. Watch trees sway in the breeze. Taste a strawberry or a pretzel. Smell coffee, cinnamon, or lemon. Your senses ground you to your environment and act as anchors when everything seems to spin. Some find it helpful to get outside and move around in the fresh air. Others feel better just sitting quietly or lying down until the episode passes. But I promise. It will pass.

If the anxiety should continue, please contact your family doctor or therapist. Talk therapy can be helpful, as well as short term use of medication.

Is it depression?

Anxiety and depression are a natural part of grief. The spirit breaking sorrow of new loss weighs heavy to the point of extreme sadness and feelings of hopelessness. This would be considered a situational depression. This isn't a clinical depression or a dysthymic disorder as the DSM V (the diagnostic manual of the American Psychiatric Association) would classify your symptoms. A depressed mood is a part of the grief we experience. It's easy for early grief to be categorized as a clinical diagnosis because the symptoms are similar. But sorrow from losing one you love is a natural human response. It's not a clinical illness. It's slow and painful. Sometimes it feels like it's never going to end. But it moves to its own place, and we learn to carry it. We integrate our loss, and life goes on. We emerge with the strength to accept loss and move forward. We're forever changed, yet able to seek happiness again. It's emotionally crippling for a time, but eventually the sun starts to show through the dark clouds. There's a return to energy and glimpses of joy start to show themselves on the horizon.

But what happens if we don't get up off the floor, never learning to take those steps? What if the dark clouds continue to darken? There's no return of energy, and joy has not given you a glimmer. This can occur in a complicated grief. Your depressed mood, so prevalent and normal in the early stages, persists and deepens. Instead of slowly beginning to move forward, you feel stuck, unable to take steps toward light. If this is the case, it can evolve into a clinical depression. If grief manifests into a depressive disorder, it's critical that you get professional treatment and support.

In March 2022, a new diagnosis of Prolonged Grief Disorder was added to the DSM-V. In a New York Times guest essay, Ellen Berry looked at its pros and cons. I have mixed feelings regarding this change. Essentially, a prolonged grief can be classified as depression, so this shift seems unnecessary. I also worry with those the author quotes that 'this designation risks pathologizing a fundamental aspect of the human experience'. It seems a shame to create a label of mental illness for those who are "actually emerging, slowly but naturally, from their losses." Ms. Berry quotes Dr. Holly Pigerson, that "it just seems like you're pathologizing love."[58]

When to seek help

While I've never been a fan of labels and diagnoses, I am a radical advocate for therapy and counseling. There are therapists who, like me, specialize in grief counseling. It's a safe place, a place of unconditional positive regard, a place of hope.

The passing of time does help. That said, you'll be sad for a long time. Even after life has gone on and you've found a place for this loss, there will be sorrow. So, when is too long? I'm very hesitant to place a time limit on your grief. It depends on who or what you're grieving, the level of trauma with your loss, how much support you have, your grief history, and if you had any history of depression prior to the loss.

There's no set standard, and I regret the psychiatric community trying to set one. It's your grief. It's your journey. All I can say is life should feel like it's moving forward again at some point. Activities of daily living and engaging with others should begin to feel natural once more. There should be more days without tears.

When these things happen depends on you and these factors mentioned previously. But it should happen. If you remain shaded by the shadow of loss, you might need to take stock. I believe if your grief has become a clinical depression you'll know. Listen to your inner voice. Trust your intuition. You'll sense if you should be feeling stronger and a bit more positive by now. If you're not, then you need to act. Or when you're still in a more active early phase of grief, and you can tell your support system is becoming weary, seek an outside ear. Either of these scenarios tell you that getting some professional help is an important next step.

There really is nothing like being able to say anything you need to say, or cry if you need to cry, or yell if you need to yell and feel emotionally safe in doing so. You don't have to worry if you said something you shouldn't have, or if someone thinks you're being weak or dramatic or silly.

It was such a relief to sit in my familiar chair in my dear therapist's sun dappled office with wooded views through every window, a sanctuary, a safe place. It felt like home, a place to grieve my son. I started seeing this gifted man soon after I started my out-patient practice. He was always there, even if five years had passed since our last visit. I'd call him when I needed him. This was the time I needed him most. Ironically, the morning I made the call was a Monday around ten a.m. – the time I found out Matthew had died just a week or so before. Being able to kick and scream and cry in this safe place likely saved many of my relationships. I can be a bit much, and I knew the emotional weight of carrying me could take its toll.

My therapist is really another of my grief stories. The last time I saw him was for a period in 2005 for a work-related issue. I sent him a few pictures of the kids and Christmas cards over the years. After retirement, relocation, and eventual return to Illinois, I was feeling like I could use a tune-up to adjust to the multiple changes and shifts that had recently occurred. When I first returned, I looked him up and found that he had retired to care for his wife who was ill. A while after, I decided to get in contact just to see if he wanted to meet for coffee, as I had done with a few of my long-term clients after retirement. I couldn't get a hold of him so Googled him and found his obituary. He had died the month before. I felt lost and abandoned for a time. But also, so grateful to have had the privilege to work with such a skilled therapist and honorable human being for so many years.

Besides the therapist's office, there are other accessible avenues of help. Most funeral homes offer grief support groups. Many hospitals do the same. There is also a program called Grief Care that many locations offer with pre-planned programs and discussion groups. Many of my clients took advantage of this group at a local church. The programs were informative. Meeting others who were also dealing with loss provided support and comfort. Social outings were often planned, and many lifelong friendships were created.

There are also support groups for specific losses. Infertility support groups are common, and some churches offer groups for abortion healing. There is a group called Compassionate Friends that provides support to parents who have lost children. And there are groups to support those who have lost a loved one by suicide. Grief is grief, but many in mourning have specific needs that can be addressed in these targeted support groups. Again, it's being with people who have suffered a similar loss, sharing their stories.

If, in reading these pages, you've decided that counseling may be right for you, I encourage you to do so. It's a valuable tool for healing. I offer some suggestions if you've never spent time with a therapist. Making the first call can be anxiety producing, and the first visit can be intimidating. I'll try to answer some of the questions you may have at the outset to ease some of this discomfort.

I've used the terms therapist and counselor interchangeably throughout this volume. Both terms refer to social workers, counselors, and psychologists with licensed credentials. While there are some differences, you can be comfortable with either. But it's important that they have experience in dealing with grief. If yours was a loss, also steeped in trauma, then it is helpful if they work also with trauma. I had a colleague who refrained from working with grieving clients. He wasn't comfortable with it. Then in one year, his mother died from surgical complications and his sister died of cancer. These life experiences opened his heart to those who grieve.

Now he knows.

So how do you find a therapist? The first step is to ask others or get a list from your insurance provider or employee assistance program for therapists they cover. You might have trusted friends or family members who have been through counseling. If not, your pastor, advisor, mentor, or primary care physician are all good resources for a referral.

Once you have names, access the website of the therapist or the group he or she is affiliated with. Most counseling practices have pictures, credentials, specialties, and brief biographies of their staff. It's important that they list loss and grief and trauma, but also note how the person looks and what they have to say. Think about who you might feel most comfortable with, taking into consideration gender, age, specialty, and practical issues, such as ease of accessibility to their office and hours they are available for appointments. There may also be something in that biography that clicks for you. A client's daughter selected a therapist from a picture and because the biography stated the therapist had never met a book she didn't like.

If you forgo the research and randomly pick a name from a local listing, you might still have a good fit. But, if you have the time, I recommend the longer route. Your journey and your needs are important. Take time to honor your pain and your desire to heal by doing your research.

Your relationship with the therapist begins with your first call to the office. Ideally, the person who answers is warm, encouraging, and gives you a positive first impression. This person will likely set up your first appointment and give you instructions regarding your initial visit. In some practices the counselors set up their own appointments. In that case, you'll be called back with an appointment time.

When you enter the office for your first appointment, you will hopefully feel comfortable and safe. There will be paperwork for you to fill out, so arrive at least fifteen minutes early so you have ample time to complete it before your appointment time.

So, what happens in the office with your therapist? It depends. We're all unique, but a few generalities exist. The paperwork you filled out needs to be reviewed. Your therapist will elaborate and answer questions about policies. Your legally protected confidentiality, and its exceptions, must be discussed before you start sharing your story.

After the routine information is done, the session generally proceeds to your chance to tell your story, along with some general screening questions. You might be one of the many clients who enter this office in acute distress. A recent death, a spouse abruptly leaving, or another traumatic event is often more emotionally charged. In those crisis situations, the therapist will simply let you talk and talk and cry and cry. I had clients who came in crisis, who never sat down, pacing throughout the whole hour. During these times, the goal of that first session will be to establish connection, listen, offer unconditional positive regard and empathy, and engender hope. Before you leave that first session, the therapist will assess your safety, and your level of support.

It's important that you be an active participant in your therapy. There aren't lab tests, x-rays or scans of your heart and mind. There aren't set protocols for specific diagnoses. Your therapist relies on you for data to make assessments. Your ability to be honest and transparent is essential. You won't help yourself if you hold back or are less than honest. Remember, this is the place where you're safe to say anything you need to say, cry all the tears you need to cry.

Forgiveness

As we journey through grief, we may find obstacles of anger, hurt, bitterness. This is especially true in complicated grief situations. Holding on to blame, shame, or guilt short circuits our natural healing. If you carry self-blame, you'll tend to hold on to your pain as a penance. You find yourself stuck in a cycle of self-punishment. The following topic of forgiveness includes whoever needs to be forgiven – the person who left you, a friend or family member, or yourself. Forgiveness is an important step in beginning to venture forward.

If you've read *Happiness Calling,* you're familiar with this exercise in forgiveness. If you're grieving the person you're still trying to forgive, it can be challenging. It's often the words you never got the chance to say, the conflict you never got to see resolved, the anger you never expressed, the hurt that never healed. A tough thing about loss is the "if onlys" and the "what ifs" that still leave bitterness on our tongue and sorrow in our heart.

The burden of unforgiven anger complicates and compounds

the intense feelings of grief. Holding on to hurt is emotionally and spiritually toxic to your efforts to heal. You might find yourself clinging to thoughts of revenge, allowing them to fuel your days. There's also a function to this. Anger feels stronger than the sorrow you carry. But the negativity creates emotional and physical stress. As you tally the toll of this burden, you'll find it's time to forgive.

Once you make the conscious decision to forgive another, it doesn't automatically happen. There aren't any magic forgiveness wands. It's a choice you make to move on from the pain. In doing so, you must re-immerse yourself into the hurt for a time. Only then, once you've looked it square in the eye, named it, and stood up to it, can you purposefully turn away.

You forgive, but you don't forget. It's impossible to erase life experiences from the brain. What has passed is ingrained and woven into who you are. You can't pull one string out of your life's delicate weaving. It's there. It happened. But by choosing forgiveness, you stop nurturing the memories, the feelings, and the pain. You quit trying to pull the string. You lay it down. You walk away, released from the toxicity it carried. You free yourself.

Forgiveness eases the soul and clears your path to healing. Deciding to forgive is the first step. If it's the person who died that needs forgiveness, there's a finality to this process, which sometimes complicates. We want to hold on to anything we have left once they're gone, even if it's anger or hurt. The feelings seem to keep them more alive in your heart.

If the person who hurt you is alive, it's like giving someone an expensive gift that you charge on a credit card. The recipient of the gift of forgiveness gets to enjoy it immediately, while you must take time to pay the debt of the decision. That debt comes in the form of soul-searching, self-honesty, and the struggle of letting go.

Forgiveness might lead to the resumption of a broken relationship. It might not. There's no requirement that you love or trust the person again. The damage may be irreparable. Letting go of pain makes you stronger. It's a choice you get to make to be rid of the burden of anger.

The following guided imagery is a tool for forgiveness.

Pick the person or persons you want to pardon. Picture a dining room – its colors, its furniture. Now look at the cluttered dining room table. You see all the memories of hurt and pain laid out there, in full view for all to see. That table hasn't been cleaned off in a long time. Every time you walk by you pick up each memory and fuel the flame.

'How could you have gone and died on me!"

"I'll never forgive him for…"

"If she hadn't lied to me, …"

"My life was ruined when he left me."

You stir up the anger and the hurt. You hold on tight, letting the poison seep in through the pores of your skin and the air you breathe. You fan the fire every day with revengeful thoughts and clenched fists.

Then comes the decision to forgive. On that day, you set a box on one of the dining room chairs. Look at all the hurt spread out on the table one more time. Then neatly place each betrayal in the box. When you've cleared the table, put the lid on the box and tie it up with ribbon. Let tears fall and feelings flow.

Take the box to the hall closet, and put it on the shelf above the coats, alongside stocking caps and plaid wool scarves, seasonal decorations, and outgrown clothes.

Now shut the door. Stand there for a minute. Sigh a long sigh. Take a deep breath and walk away from that closet that now holds all the pain. Dust and polish the now empty dining room table. Add a nice runner and a vase of fresh flowers. The table is clean and shining now, ready to be used for better things than holding pain.

Each time you open the closet, you might glance up at the box. You have a catch in your breath and experience a tick of the old hurt. You say "Oh, I remember all that from my past." But you won't take it down. It's put away. The tick will fade. You close the closet door and go on about your day.

This exercise can also be applied to yourself. You may find there are things you haven't forgiven yourself for in your relationship with your loved one. It might be directly related to his death. Words you didn't say, actions you feel you could've done to save him. You feel you could've been a better friend, spouse, sibling. Find that self-blame and go through this same mental imagery exercise. Pick it up, examine it, and then put it away.

In "No Hard Feelings", the Avett Brothers hope to:

Walk through the night, straight to the light,
Holding the love I've known in my life
And no hard feelings.

I hope this is a goal we all aspire to achieve before we leave this earth.

What does moving beyond your grief look like?

Declaring yourself healed from grief is a tenuous claim. I couldn't offer a lifeline of hope if I didn't believe in healing. But I also know that grief never truly goes away. Sorrow can emerge at any time. At first, on the healing spectrum, it will feel like you're immersed and drowning with no reprieve, no escape. As time goes on, there will be minutes, then hours, then days that you'll feel okay. As your journey turns into months and years, the time between the sorrow will expand. You may go months without feeling the sorrow, but then a song you shared grabs you by the ankle and pulls you under. Only this time you know you'll come back up to the surface, gasping a breath of the present and, after tears and remembering, it will be okay. The times you feel the pain will be intense but of shorter duration. Some call it moving on. Some call it moving in. I call it healing. In that healing, a part of our soul moves over and makes room for it. It's the kind of human healing that leaves a scar, or a limp, that might leave a daily reminder of what you've lost. But it's a healing, just the same. Loss finds a place in our fabric, a fine piece of golden silk thread that shines in our heart's tapestry. The loss integrates into our soul, and we breathe it, and it beats in our heart.

It's hard to let go of grief for many reasons. First, it takes so much energy to endure the sorrow. As we take steps forward, we carry that heavy load with us as we trudge back to life as it now is. It's exhausting, mentally, emotionally, and physically. That's one of the reasons the self-care is so important. Your body and soul have experienced a trauma. It requires the same basic life healing you would need if you had a serious illness or injury. You need rest, care, nutrition, and all the other ingredients to heal.

Once that primal need of biological recovery is resolved, other factors emerge as roadblocks that must be maneuvered to get to the other side.

We may fear letting go of our grief. So, we hold on. With my clients, there was sometimes an underlying fear that if they let go of grief, they would lose their loved one. The grief, the constant pain and sorrow, was all they had left. It was a connection that was too scary to let go of. What if she forgot what he looked like? What if he forgot the sound of her voice? The grief was the last tangible link. Our work focused on what to hold on to and what to let go of. What would life without sorrow look like? Processing the fear allowed them to find ways to stay connected to loved ones. This was a personal journey, but each discovered that you don't arrive at a spiritual connection until you've let go of the earthly link.

Another reason we hold on to grief is guilt. There's a part of us, deep down in our being, that feels like we're being disloyal if we move forward without them. Facing that guilt and its components is a major factor in healing. There might be true guilt or shame to deal with, but often it's that sense of abandonment of our loved one. Talking about this, and addressing it through letters or journaling, is helpful. This allows us to go about the business of finding a spiritual way to maintain a connection without suffering every day.

These conflicts are often present if a widow begins to think about dating. Some couples have the time to talk about this while both are still alive, and they know what their spouse or partner wanted for them. If couples had the depth of relationship to discuss these tender topics, they were more likely to share that they wanted their partner to go on and have a full life with another. If that conversation took place, it makes it easier to move forward. But it invariably feels risky to set out on a new romantic path.

At the other end of this spectrum are those left behind who can't be alone. This is not an indictment of those survivors. It's just a fact. Many of us do not want to be alone. Whether this be from life experiences or early learning, it's a common factor in early remarriages or becoming involved in a new relationship quickly. While it might be best for the widow or widower, it often leads to some negative ramifications from family and friends who believe their parent or friend is "still warm in the grave" and the partner is starting up with someone new. This can lead to unnecessary conflict if there isn't open, honest communication between family and friends.

Spiritual connection

What about the spiritual connection? It's available to all of us. I can't tell you what it looks like or even how to achieve it. But I know it happens. That might sound a bit out there, and you may begin to think that I'm advocating seances and the like. No judgement if you want to, but what I'm talking about is a dawning of an understanding that we're linked to our loved one in more than just this earthly life. Our shared life experiences and love leave us with connections that goes beyond them sitting in the chair beside us.

How many of you have sensed the presence of your loved one? How many have heard a whisper in your ear? Smelled a perfume? Found a "gift" they've left behind? When I make Christmas cookies, I feel my grandmother's presence in the kitchen. When I go back to my hometown for a visit, I drive by the Redi-mix plant my dad managed. I'll sit there in my car by the bins of sand and gravel, and I feel him there. Not long after my son died, I felt his tiny, perfect hand on my cheek. There's a McDonalds my grandpa and I always stopped at when I picked him up from the train. He'd have a cheeseburger and coffee, and we'd have our moments alone before family noise took over at home. I feel his presence whenever I drive by that restaurant. These moments come when we let them come. If we continue to be in denial of their death, we can't be open to these moments. Those who have died can also visit us in our dreams. The tough ones are when we dream that they're still alive, and we wake up and discover it was only a dream, and cry and cry. But other times dreams can be comforting. We wake up feeling that our person or pet is still with us on another plane. Cardinals are said to be spiritual messengers from God and loved ones watching over us. Occasionally, I notice a cardinal being particularly active just outside my window. These visits can come when I'm feeling good, but especially during times of stress. I'll look out there and a feeling of peace will come over me. And I wonder who it is that's covering me today. And I say thank you. White feathers have also brought me a sense of connection as they represent angels watching over us. Each found white feather becomes a special treasure.

In Donna Ashworth's poem "Last Night" she writes:

I can't guarantee any of this is real, but I remain open to it always. It's the same as being open to something on the other side of death, whether it be Heaven or another plane of reality beyond the veil. I don't think we can discount anything as possibility. For every scientific statement that none of these things are valid, there is a story that makes denial difficult.

While there's much in the spiritual realm that remains unseen and mystical, there are also many earthbound methods of keeping memories alive. After all, memories are full of promise. Whether that be through a spiritual connection or a cookie recipe or a stuffed ducky, the links are strong and sustaining.

How do we hold memories?

Many answers to this question are scattered throughout different grief stories. But others still randomly come to mind from my history and that of others. Families often create a memorial that reflects a passion or special cause of their loved ones. Many special events such as golf tournaments, commemorative runs, walks, and benefits are created to honor and remember. I recently attended a benefit for a local family's son who died some years ago in an auto accident. It's called Plots for Drew – a fundraiser to raise money for those who can't afford burial expenses.

There's a run/walk that you may be aware of called Susan G. Komen Race for the Cure. It took place annually all over the country to celebrate and remember those we lost to breast cancer and to honor the survivors. What you may not know is that Susan was a resident of Peoria and is buried here. She was a thirty-two-year-old wife and mother from a prominent Peoria family who died of breast cancer in the early eighties. Her sister began the race in Dallas where she was living, and Peoria's race was the second oldest. This event has raised millions of dollars for breast cancer research.

Like everything else, the race was a victim of COVID. It has now transitioned to the name Komen More Than Pink Walk and was held this year on its traditional Saturday before Mother's Day.

My heart remembers its early days. I couldn't make it through the event without tears – so many survivors in pink t-shirts surrounded by, back then, female friends and loved ones. It took on even more emotional significance as my mother was diagnosed twice and my friends began to face the challenge. There were pink weatherproof papers the size of race bibs that said, "I'm racing in Memory of" or "I'm racing in Celebration of." Race participants printed names on the pages and pinned them to the back of their shirts. Those pages were practically full the last time I wore mine. There was a special magazine included in the race goodie bags with articles by survivors and local writers. I was honored to have essays included. Race For the Cure was both a community memorial and a personal pilgrimage that brought a tribe together, honoring everyone breast cancer touched. In those days of women only, the husbands, fathers, sons, and friends lined the race route with signs and music and shouts of encouragement. My mother came to Illinois early enough one year to walk in the race with me and her then three-year-old granddaughter. She was so empowered by the event. She was tough. She was a survivor. In the annual survivor's picture – a sea of pink under an arch of pink balloons - she has a loud smile and her arm raised in a fisted salute.

Another way I remember is by visiting my roots. My hometown was a village of parents and grandparents. There was no getting away with anything because any parent who saw you held you accountable. No. We weren't angels and did figure out, as teens, how to get by with a few misbehaviors. But all the families being so present in each other's lives, gave a sense of safety and sureness. So now, when most of that parent generation has died, the times we're together takes on a special meaning, that I hadn't anticipated. I've always enjoyed my class reunions – forty plus of us who knew each other since kindergarten. But as we got older, I realized I cherished being around these others who knew my family, who knew my red-headed mom was a hot-head, who knew my dad was crushed on by all the girls, who knew how special it was when we got to ride my bus driver grandpa's fan bus to games, who knew my grandmother's work calloused hands could also nurse the tiniest abandoned kitten. These people had been to sleepovers, vacations, and teen parties where we all got in trouble. They remembered my mom with toilet paper wrapped hair and robe waiting for us in the driveway on a late for curfew night, or Dad letting us ride in the back of his Ranchero around town just to check on some boys' whereabouts. They remembered that they could talk my grandparents into anything, and that all the ice cream in the grocery store freezer was ours to eat. They shared my history, and I shared theirs. One of my sweetest ways to remember my family is through these connections with this tribe filled with my history. They knew. They hold my sweet, evocative memories, understanding the sacredness we share.

Memorial Day used to also be called Decoration Day, a day to decorate graves of loved ones and friends. This tradition, sadly, seems to be dying with my parent's generation. But there was a time when we believed that peonies bloomed in late May specifically to be used for family graves. When I see the peonies start to bud, my instinctive thoughts go to the cemetery where I found myself every year. My in-laws traveled all over the state delivering flowers to graves. Even after my father-in-law could barely walk, he still remembered his family who had passed. I have a cousin who continues the tradition of taking care of my family's graves, all in the country cemetery outside my hometown. I don't know who will follow her. Likely, all my family will be remembered in other ways, but no more peonies on Decoration Day. What have I done to compensate for not attending to my loved one's graves on a regular basis? I use my perennial gardens to remember them – a rose that my grandma loved, Dad's favorite-colored tulips, Matthew's redbud tree, my mother-in-law's peach tea rose, the Rose of Sharon. There's a memory for everyone scattered somewhere in the garden, and as my eyes rest on each, my heart remembers.

Heather Brammeier, Bradley University Art Professor and sculptor and installation artist uses her art to memorialize her loved ones' lives and their impact on her own. She has a series of installations about love and loss, in which she works through the death of her first husband and her mother, and the separation from a second husband years later. Her latest installation in the series, titled 'She Kept these Things', reconsiders "the past, present, and future. Our relationship with our memories changes over time, and we have the agency to frame memories in ways that help to process loss so that grief is not debilitating."[61]

There are families who declare a celebration on their loved one's birthday, or wedding anniversary, or any date that carries significance. Some, especially with large families, have a whole day of partying – a family reunion in honor of Mom or Dad or Sister or Brother. It creates a time to gather, to remember, to tell stories, to mark a legacy, to celebrate a life.

How many of you have saved a voicemail or your loved one's voicemail recording? There's something about hearing a voice. It connects in our brain with presence. The sound of a voice now gone makes us sad, brings tears, but also offers a degree of comfort. In that twenty second message, there's a life force.

Think about your memories and how you've memorialized your special people who have died. How do you keep them present in your heart? I'd love to hear about your special testimonials to those you've loved and lost.

Legacy

Whether we live to old age in relatively good health, or are called to leave this earth too soon, we leave a legacy behind. I'm not speaking about how much money you will to others, or the special locket you give to your daughter. I'm talking about how you'll be remembered. What mark will you leave on the world? What stories of your life will future generations hear?

In our youth, we tend to focus on legacies of greatness. I planned on being a photojournalist covering the Vietnam War and, after that, a great poet. I'm sure you've thought of some greatness in your future. Of course, there are those of us who will cure disease and purvey the planets, but most of us will live simple lives. As we get older our circle gets smaller. We begin to understand that if we want to leave the world a better place, it must be done one person at a time. It starts with our little corner of this grand and wonderful planet - family, friends, neighbors, the community in which we live. If we each focus on our small sphere of influence, it really can become a better world.

When an elderly friend was stricken with terminal cancer, she wondered at all the people who came to visit, who sent gifts, cards, and prayers. She said she couldn't understand it. She'd lived such an ordinary life. But the reality was, she'd lived an extraordinary life. She had quietly cared for others, freely giving of herself to family, neighbors, and church family. She was kind, honest, generous, and humble – tireless in her generosity.

When February came, and she was nearing her time to leave this earth, my young daughter and I took her flowers and a Valentine my daughter made. In all that was going on in her life, she took the time to write a thank-you note to my daughter. That thoughtfulness was such a natural part of her that she never thought twice about making the effort. That note became a part of her legacy carried on in a little girl's heart.

People stand out in our life. There are three lovely souls who cushioned me, shaped me, inspired me - my grandmother, my parents' friend Sharon, and my freshman high school English teacher. They each gave me a gift. Grandma gave me security and safety and unconditional love. Sharon gave me eyes to see the rest of the world filled with culture and beauty beyond a small Illinois farming community. My teacher taught me to believe I could do anything if I put my mind to it. He said, "Aim for the stars."

My grandmother's legacy was that of service, loyalty, and dedication – and love. In her later years, she was ravaged by a disease that eventually took her. By then, I was old enough to appreciate who she was as a woman – not just as my grandma (though that would've been enough). I saw her continue to do her job as a small-town newspaper editor for as long as she could, keeping her promises and commitments to the community she loved. But most of all, I remember a grandmother who cherished her great-grandchildren, still toddlers at the time. She leaned on Grandpa to walk, but when the "boys" arrived, the orders were to help her get down on the floor to play. And play she did – trucks, Legos, blocks, Candyland.

My parent's friend, Sharon, died last week. This story is a fitting last addition to these pages. She was a person I wish I'd visited more in later years, but she always knew I loved her. Remember to follow through on those loving thoughts. She is in both of my books. In Happiness Calling, she's the person who took me to see The Sound of Music in Chicago when I was twelve, opening a whole new world of music and the arts. In this book, she is the family friend who stood at the ER door quietly shaking her head telling me that my dad was dead. She was a woman filled with life and love. I'm fortunate to have her as one of my angels.

My teacher was the first "bigger than life" person I met. Brimming with confidence and tenacity, he was a shining star in our small town. Some folks loved him. Others loved to hate him. He went on to reach his own goals as both college and NBA basketball coach. He lived boldly far beyond our small town. But in his first teaching job, he believed in an awkward fourteen-year-old writer and taught her to do the same.

When I think back, those who remain in my heart were people like my friend, my teacher, and my grandmother. They lived by example and did the best they could with what they had been given. It was the simple lives of the honorable souls who did their best that dictated who I wanted to be "when I grew up."

As you think about your legacy, begin a vision board of how you want it to look. This could include the kindnesses you want to act on, the things you want to teach your children and your grandchildren, the spiritual gifts you hope to leave, the memories of those you loved – a visual reminder of how you want to be remembered. Take a few minutes now to pause with that thought. How do you want to be remembered? Whose hearts do you want to be woven into? What threads do you want to weave? Threads of love? Threads of peace? Threads of wonder? Threads of service? We can't guarantee that these will bear fruit, but we can prepare the foundation of possibility by the life we live today.

As we've journeyed through this book together, it's become clear that how we grieve and how we view our own mortality are deeply intertwined. With that in mind, I'd like you to take part in a last assignment. I'd like you to write your eulogy. This is a powerful tool in processing your own death one day. Write it based on the life you're living and prepare it as if you're going to stand up and share it with others at your funeral. Keep it in your special drawer. It's another living document that will change and grow. Periodically, compare it to your legacy vision board. Do they align? Are they a consistent depiction of the life you want to live and how you want to be remembered? If not, you have time to adjust.

Final thoughts

What a journey we've shared.

Remember you and everyone you've loved are unique and precious. A mere grain of sand in the universe? Yes, but the universe manifests meaning for each grain of sand. The opening words of "Desiderata" by Max Ehrmann tell us "You are a child of the universe no less than the trees and the stars; you have a right to be here. And whether it is clear to you, no doubt the universe is unfolding as it should."[62]

There's peace in those words, while still creating questions. Does it mean that everything happens for a reason, that there's some master plan that unfolds? Does it mean we each have a destiny, a pre-ordained time to depart this earth? Does it mean that the universe has a place for us after we leave this earthly plane? These mysteries of life and death go beyond our human scope of understanding. What I do know is that the circle of life goes on. We find joy. We find shooting stars of love that blaze in our heart, no matter how briefly. We find productivity. We find peace. And at the time of our death, I believe we find the answers. When our loved ones died, they gazed beyond this earthly vision and saw the answers. They found a peace we'll never know on earth. Believing that sustains and offers solace. I grieve for myself and what I've lost, but I know those I loved are in a sacred space. We'll all get there one day.

On the last page of *What We Wish Were True*, Tallu Schuyler Quinn lists "Some of what it might be like: It might be I'm a waxy leaf, rushing downstream, following the curve of the water, flipping, tumbling, somersaulting the watershed, a delight in the water…Or maybe I will be cosmic. A ball of light, a star in the night sky, obvious and out loud. Wayfinding, unapologetic, shooting. Or maybe I will be a song, golden words rolling off of someone's tongue, a tune anyone can hum. Or maybe I will be the ear who hears it…Maybe we become all of this and more."[63]

But while you're earthbound with me, continue your healing. Take time to laugh when you can and always love. Through your pain, keep your senses open. See the good in all. Be fully present. As Warren Zevon wisely suggested, "Enjoy every sandwich." Live each day as if it's a precious gift because it is. We don't know when it will be our last. Work at accepting moments as impermanent gifts. Don't hold on too tight. In wanting it all to last forever, we miss the moments of bliss that create life's rhythm. Even in light of sorrow, don't discount fleeting ecstatic moments. Never miss a chance for love, for connection. These moments warm our heart and flush our cheeks, leaving a sweet taste on the tongue and a lifetime of memories.

Share your gifts with others and be open to what others teach you. Keep your eyes open. Notice. Be a part of this lovely, messy, quirky, wise human village.

I leave you gifts of understanding. You now have a skill-filled toolbox for healing. Use it as needed along the way. Use your grief timeline. It's a living document. Return to it and make additions as memories and feelings arise. Remember it can be basic or as creative as you like, incorporating illustrations and art. It's a map of your grief journey. It's the story of exquisite richness that comes from love and loss. Grief reflects how much we loved during this earthly adventure. Your life is a gathering place for all that you've experienced – the good, the bad, the heartbreaking, and the joyful. To erase any of that is to erase a part of you. You wouldn't be who you are right here, right now, without every trace of the life you've lived. Would we like to avoid pain, have crippling grief taken from us? Yes. But to be free of sorrow is to be devoid of love.

Loss may profoundly change us, but so does love. The grief you experience is a testament to the treasures of your time with your loved one - of having loved deeply. You were changed by the time spent together, no matter how brief. Rest in the joy that time brought to your heart, the richness it brought to your soul, and the sweetness of memories that remain.

May you find contentment that comes from a life of meaning with golden threads of what you've lost interwoven into treasured fabric. Open your heart to authentic relationships that bring you joy.

I hope by hearing my story and writing your own you've found new understanding, new tools and renewed courage. Over time, you'll begin to put one foot back in front of the other, walking again, but in a different world - emerging with peace to accept loss and move forward. Forever changed, emotionally crippled for a time, but you will go on. The darkness lifts. Energy returns, and you're able to enjoy life again.

I promise things get better. But during the inevitable moments that you lose hope, rely on someone who has hope for you. Let the people you trust lead you through the darkest days.

Healing starts in glimmers caught at the corner of your eye – with fleeting moments of light, like a glorious hint of hope. Slowly, glimmers turn into moments of peace, then hours of lightness. Eventually entire days will pass free of shadow.

Time helps us heal. We are adaptive beings. The mind and the heart will assimilate change and find a place to put the pain. Our heart will grow around it until the loss becomes golden, glistening threads of our soul. Honor the time it takes. And always hold on to hope.

In the Introduction, I mentioned my difficulty writing a book about grief. That remains true, but as the writing progressed, I realized this is another step in my own journey. In writing Surviving Grief, I found strength I hadn't anticipated, and a humility that softened me. It has been one of the great honors of my life to share this journey with you. Thank you.

APPENDIX A: ESSAYS AND POEMS

I want to share these related essays, poems, and op-eds because they offer a window into how healing progressed for me and others. Some are excerpts because portions of the content were used in the text of the book. Others are in their entirety.

The first poem relates to Part III – What We Grieve. I wrote this for Matthew some years after he died.

"To Matthew"

Matthew's feet were perfect.
All ten tiny toes were there.
His newborn shoulders were downy soft.
He had his big brother's red hair.
Yet, as I kissed him into the world, I tearfully whispered good-bye.
Matthew would not feel the sun on his face. He would never utter a cry.
He went to rest on a country hill as the clouds wept for my pain.
I offered his dreams to the wind, his unsung songs to the rain.
For weeks I rocked a teddy in his nursery not meant to be,
And sang soft silent lullabies to the smile I would never see.
Many years have since passed since my Matthew was born,
His first steps never taken, and no first Christmas morn.
Yet I find he's always with me in my heart and soul so blessed.
His laughter rustles the Autumn leaves. The blazing sunset is his bequest.
There's a guardian angel named Matthew. If there is a doubt in your heart
somewhere,
Watch his brothers and sister come home each day and shake angel dust
from their hair.

Next is an excerpt of an op-ed published in the *Peoria Journal Star*, April 2000. This also relates to Part III – What We Grieve.

"A Life Never Lived: Mother Mourns Child, Celebrates Memory, Joy He Brought to Her Heart."

My family celebrated a birthday last month. There was the usual cake, candles, and singing of Happy Birthday. The gift was a bright blue balloon infused with enough helium for very high flying so it would make it to Heaven. This magical balloon was inscribed with messages from family. It was for Matthew who only knows celestial birthdays.

Nine years ago, we said goodbye to him before saying hello. Matthew never saw our faces, or the sunshine, or snowflakes. He never held his teddy bear, played football with his brothers, or teased his little sister. Matthew spent his eight months of life in the warmth and illusory safety of my womb. The video that chronicles his life is a sonogram where he swims, and plays, and waves. That's it.

On a brisk sunny day in March, we brought him into this world aware that he had already left us behind. We held him and rocked him and told him we loved him. Then we laid him to rest on a hill in the country where birds sing to little boys.

This is another essay written about reproductive grief from Part III – What We Grieve. It was originally published in *Healthy Cells Magazine*, January 2002.

"A Time for Every Season"

There is a time for every season. We see that Biblical truth in our own lives every day. There is a certain predictability and expected rhythm to the way the seasons of life flow. The earthly script reads winter, spring, summer, and fall. The generally ascribed schedule to human life on earth is we are born, we mature to adulthood, we mate, procreate, raise our offspring, age, and die. If all goes well, each will be a fulfilling and fruitful period from which we learn many things. Just as the seasons of the earth, each has its purpose – its reason for being. As a species we are drawn on to the next stage via some natural antenna that creates the yearning to move on.

Having made it, hopefully, only halfway through my journey, I have experienced the ebb and flow of my own humanity. I was late in the procreating phase, beginning to wonder if that "biological clock" was going to kick my maternal instincts into gear. When it finally occurred the yearning for a child took me by storm, completely caught off guard by the intensity and sheer joy of the dreams that began to consume my being. When I held that tiny miracle of creation (who is now driving a real car) in my arms for the first time, his life had been dreamed in vivid Technicolor and surround sound a million times in my heart and mind. His life began for me the moment I felt the pull of motherhood on my heart signaling the onset of that season of life.

My season of procreation held many blessings. Some I got to keep. Others God is storing in Heaven. Now in the process of raising the offspring placed in my charge for their earthly life, I also still miss the two God already has. Our baby boy died in my womb a mere month away from my arms. Another angel is much tinier having only been a part of me for eight weeks. The wisdom I carry on from these losses affects how I cherish my living children. It also impacts my work as I have a heart for the often-unrecognized grief of parents with empty arms. Whether neonatal, perinatal, or prenatal, the grief is there, and the arms still ache. Each one of my five children holds a place in my heart, a time in my history, a place in my memory. Each had a life in my dreams even before they were conceived. When that dream is taken by infertility or early loss, it doesn't diminish the pain of the abruptness of a dream being snatched from us.

The loss of a child is tragic, the greatest pain we could ever endure in this life. We sometimes tend to forget those who lose children before they become real to others on the outside. It is important to remember that a pre-birth loss is just as much a reality to the parents of that wee creation. The couple experiencing miscarriage in the first few weeks is left to grieve that minute of presence.

Each is real and palpable pain and sorrow. We need to remember this in how we respond to these hearts. Reassuring clichés and platitudes don't cut it. Don't minimize the loss. Give it validation. Remember the dream. Give the same understanding and kindness you would ascribe to any loss. Let your heart be free to carry the hurt for part of their journey. Support them and nurture, to give the strength to try again. For this is the season of their lives for which God has many blessings. God's blessings come in many shapes and forms – one of which may be you.

- This is an excerpt of the poem I wrote about aging, relating to Loss of Self in Part III – What We Grieve. It was performed in April 2015 at Peoria Contemporary Arts Center.

"The Sixty-five Jive"

So, this is it – old age, the end stage. Some call it twilight or golden.

I call it another day of my mission in transition, my two-thirds through. Who knew?

In a two-thirds life crisis I hit the wall when I thought of it all still left on my list.

Only so many do-overs remain of sunshine without rain, in the forecast of the last one third.

At twenty-nine I pictured aging, then forgot about it, til now and the sixty-five jive

Fully alive, perusing what I'm losing, yet what I get to keep.
As the cream rises to the top, and I take sips, taste it on my lips,
And find the best is right on the tip of my tongue - old or young.
So, I'll embrace my age, my place on the stage…
The family will visit whenever able.
We'll laugh and eat at the dining table with history etched in the surface.
I'll garden and sew and appreciate art, treasuring each new day's start.
And sit in afternoon sunbeams in the front porch rocker,
Nuzzling cat ears — napping some as I softly hum music that makes me smile.

Until one sunshine afternoon the humming will drift off
And the cat will glance up as the nuzzling wanes. And the sun will set.

The following essay relates to Divorce and Other Relationship Fractures in Part III – What We Grieve. It is unpublished. It's about a confusing night during my divorce in the late 70's.

"The Night Denial Stopped"

It's Saturday night at the Old Susannah, a bar/restaurant on the edge of town. My mother and I sit in the red vinyl booth across from each other. It's 1977. We're celebrating my divorce from the "slime bag, good for nothing" who done me wrong. The songs of Charlie Daniels and George Jones play on the jukebox. Though it's still the dinner hour, the evening's band — two farm boys with guitars and a townie on drums — is setting up on the corner stage, an indoor/outdoor carpeted platform. The knotty pine paneled walls are lit by the fake Tiffany lights hanging over the booths, giving the whole scene a golden haze.

I've come to this restaurant since I was a child. It's a strange combination of family diner/country bar/pick-up joint that was the scene of many birthday, anniversary, family, and pre-high school dance dinners of my youth. The fried chicken is the best in the county. They serve hush puppies and corn on the cob family-style. The beer is cold. That's pretty much all you need on a Saturday night in small town Illinois.

I consider myself more urbane now, living in the big city of 110,000 a few miles west, but when I come home — it's home. This place returns me to my roots as certainly as sleeping in my old bedroom or snuggling the family dog.

So here I sit, once again, with Mom. We toast to the future, and good riddance. We offer a moment of silence as she says, "I'm glad your dad didn't have to see this. He would've killed the little prick." The mention of Dad always quiets us for a moment. It's only been three years since his Chevy El Camino threw itself under a semi with Daddy at the wheel. We squint our tears back in and take a drink of beer. "To Dad," I say, noticing mom's lack of return toast. We reminisce about how he always mistrusted my husband of seven years. It was written off that there was never going to be anyone good enough for his princess, but...

Johnny Tillotson croons out a tune. He's always been one of Mom's favorites, so we stop to sing along. Then we get back to the business of two-timing husband bashing. We order rhubarb pie with our next beers. We talk about my bright future in nursing and the interesting brother of my best friend. I've got the whole world ahead of me. Life is good.

Cara, our waitress, is a second-grade teacher by day. We've known each other forever. She shows up now with our check and a free Brandy Alexander. She gives me a hug, and I'm surrounded with a cloud of Heaven Scent perfume. "You're gonna' be fine," she whispers in my ear.

Mom and I are winding down and yawning. We swear we'll never eat again. Fat and happy, we relax and wait for the next tune. Ray Price starts to sing, and I innocently listen, unsuspecting of what's to come. "Lay your head upon my pillow," I smiled and told Mom I love this song. I closed my eyes, listening to the lyrics with the backdrop hum of conversation and laughter.

Then the words started to be more focused. "And make believe you love me one more time for the good times." A strange sort of hiccup came up in my chest. A chuckle? A giggle? I don't know what it started as, but it became an emesis of emotion. All at once, my heart wrenched and twisted and squeezed to a point of no breath. "Don't look so sad, I know it's over." A great gasp of breath erupted as a sob. "I'll be there if you should find you ever need me." My face crumbled and fell into my hands. I cried and cried and cried until there were no more tears. No more sobs. No more hiccups. No more.

All the bravado and optimism fell to the wayside as the reality of the loss of seven years and a man I thought I would spend the rest of my life with rolled over me and left me a wasteland of weeping. I let all the hurt of his betrayal pound in my ears rendering me deaf to everything but the roar of my wailing and the words of the song. I wanted to pound the table screaming, "How could he do this to me!!" over and over. At the same time, I yearned to curl up in a ball on the seat of the booth and mew and whimper and wither away.

The song ended. Mom sat there helpless and bewildered. The band was tuning up. The jukebox was now silent. The chatter around us continued. No one was aware that I had just been laid bare and stripped of denial. I sat up, dried my face and arms and hands of tears with rough paper napkins from the booth dispenser. Mom asked me if I was ok. For the first time in the last six months, I could answer honestly. 'No, I'm not ok. I'm sick with hurting. I'm devastated and lost. I miss him and hate him. I love him and want to castrate him. I feel physically ill from the pain in my heart and soul.'

She sat there helplessly. She took my hand. Mom was used to me being the strong one. Now, she wasn't quite sure what to do with me. So, we just sat there and held hands. And that was what I needed.

It was time to go. The party had gone on without us. We left the golden glow, walking into the night. It had started to rain - gentle and lonesome. My hair dampened to my forehead as I walked slowly to the car, words vibrated in my heart. "Hear the whisper of the raindrops blowing soft against the window — and make believe you love me one more time." The hurting had begun.

This essay relates to For the Children in Divorce and Other Fractures, Part III – What We Grieve. It was originally published as an op-ed in the *Peoria Journal Star*, 1999

"A Child's Plea: Stay Together, Mom and Dad"

"What follows is a note to Mom and Dad, a compilation of the little and big voices I have heard in my twenty years as a therapist.

Dear Mom and Dad,

You tell me breaking up my family, my stability, my identity is best for me. It sounds so sacrificial and selfless, yet why do I feel so bad? Shouldn't I feel good if you're doing this to protect me? Why is it I can only think of coming down to breakfast and Daddy not being there? Or never again have a Christmas Eve listening to the murmur of your voices as I pretend to sleep. I can't help but think of all the times I've seen you two laugh together. That sound was always like angels singing. Your eyes would get all crinkly and you would kind of be like magnets having to touch. And I would think in my heart, "Someday, I'm going to love somebody like that." Then there were the times when we were so sad, like when Grandma died. We held each other and prayed. It was safe and warm inside your hugs. No matter what pain was just outside, I knew we could make it through. You healed each other, and because of that I got healed.

How, now can you tell me you don't love each other anymore? How can I believe in love if you quit? How can I believe anything lasts if all that I thought would last forever is gone? And will you continue to love me? You promise you'll never stop, that it's a different kind of love that doesn't end. Didn't you promise to never stop loving each other too, no matter what happens, whether you got sick or poor or have problems? Well, you broke your promise to each other. Why should I think that you will keep your promise to me?? I just figure a day will come when I do just enough wrong that I'll be left behind too.

You tell me now that you're divorced, you get along better. I can't help but wonder if you had tried harder at being married, you might have gotten along better then, too. You say it's easier apart. For who? Not for me! I'm the one with two rooms and two families. I'm the one who needs a sweater or book that's at the other house. I'm the one who is always having to meet your new "friends." I'm the one who misses sleepovers, ballgames, or just standing around talking after school because I'm not at the right house at the right time. If you get along better after divorcing, why do you still get in arguments? And why do you tell me about them? I feel like I must choose sides. I don't want to hear how my mom's a bad housekeeper. I don't want to hear about how my dad can't make enough money and is cheating me out of my child support.

And what about when I'm grown? I pray that you can get along at the important times. I don't want to have to look in two different directions at my graduation. I want you both sitting there on the aisle during the recessional. I don't want to have to worry about who is sitting where or who is angry at whom if I am silly enough to ever plan a wedding. I don't want to have to manipulate holiday dinners. This never ends, does it?

I just want warm hugs and kisses, and to wake up and have everything be the same again. You may have thought it was awful. I thought it was the best. Being at home with my mom and dad on a Saturday night, watching a movie and eating popcorn, is my dream. Hearing my dad's laugh and smelling Mom's perfume at the same time is my dream. Seeing you smile at each other is my dream. Feeling like love lasts forever is my dream.

Love,
Your Child of Divorce

This is an untitled poem I wrote when I was a child sometime in the early sixties, also For the Children, Divorce and Other Fractures.

Isn't there any way for me to be able to help them.
Why can't I bring back closeness?
The way it's always been.
It seems different this time, there's a feeling of conclusion.
No words of reassurance and no secure illusion.
I think this is the end-The end to all I've known.

There will no longer be a family, No more happy home.
There will be no waiting for him to come home at night - No supper time
discussions.
Instead of being one of three, I'll now be one of two.
The loneliness will be here, and there's nothing I can do.
What is there that I can say to make them change their mind?
Can't there be that love again? Is it so hard to find?
Now I find I'm helpless - no use — it's now too late.
Words cannot be taken back- Why do they have to separate?

This is an op-ed for the *Peoria Journal Star* one year after 9/11, titled "Honor the Heroes, Memorialize the Lost, Heal, Go On". It relates to National Grief in Part III – What We Grieve.

When we are crippled by pain, it doesn't matter who is holding us up or whose burden you carry. Tragedy brings understanding that we are all one at some visceral level. Once the crisis is over, we become uncomfortable with that degree of intimacy and must shake it off and pull away. But anniversaries bring us together again. We connect with memories of where, when, and why. We hold onto heroes of policemen, firemen and the rescue workers who remind us of collective courage and valor. Recovery occurs, but I don't know if any of us will ever feel as safe as we once did. The fear that it could happen again, flutters somewhere, in the shadows of my heart…. We commemorate the heroes and memorialize the lost. We heal and we go on — almost.

APPENDIX B: WRITING PROMPTS

I've tried to include all the prompts from the text in this list to make it more convenient for you to track. They are listed by book section. Since each section discusses different forms of grief and issues that surround it, they won't automatically read as your grief story. When looking back over your notes, they might seem a bit random. But as you continue, you'll discover what parts are of value to you and your journey. Those will become your grief story.

Introduction

I suggest you get a notebook to keep notes on these reflections. I'm partial to beautiful things so I'd recommend a blank journal in your favorite color that feels soft to your hand. Also, a special pen, like a fountain pen would be nice. But if these aren't available to you, any loose-leaf paper, spiral notebook, or a sturdy roll of paper towels will do. It's your notes that are important.

Your timeline and grief story are living documents that you'll likely add to as memories of other losses rise to the surface. Keep your timeline in a special drawer with your journal, to be pulled out as needed. When you've finished a first read of Surviving Grief, put it in the drawer also.

The timeline and the notes you'll make throughout the chapters, might be the beginning of your story in detail, or it may remain the whole story. That's up to you. I've found for myself and clients, that it's helpful to take what you've written a step further by organizing and writing your story in more depth.

Part I:
Communal Denial
Take a minute with your journal to think about a time when

you knew someone was going to die. How were you different? How did you feel about it? Do you think it changed how you grieved in any way?

Grief and the Arts

Spend a few minutes to reflect. Think about what movies, books, or songs stand out in your heart. What scenes or lyrics, when thought of, immediately brings a burning rush of tears. Then think about why. Write about the "why" in your journal.

Quantifying Grief

Look at your perceptions of loss and what quantifiers you carry. This is an important entry to your journal. Being able to face a bit of your own underbelly of judgement is valuable for your growth. You may also find a new level of empathy developing from this.

Part II: So Much Sadness

The Sweater

Take a few minutes to focus on how you're feeling right now in your own grief, in reference to Kubler-Ross's stages. Don't go beyond the now – not backward or ahead. Tomorrow you might feel different. This morning you may have felt different. But it's the right now that matters. Think about the stages. Where are you? Write a couple sentences on the subject in your journal. From this point forward, take a minute at the end of each day. Think about where you are and write it in your notebook.

Days of Loss -the first days

With notebook in hand, take a few minutes to reflect on your most difficult loss. What do you remember of those early days? Who do you remember? What did your first steps toward healing look like?

Part III: What We Grieve

Your grief story

With the journal entries you've done, you've already begun notes for your grief story. Now we take the first steps of organizing it. We begin by creating a timeline. This is done, simply, with a horizontal line across a sheet, or sheets, of paper and marking your history with vertical notations along the line. Regular copy paper is all you need, (or that trusty paper towel roll), making your line parallel to the longest edge. If you need more than one piece of paper, tape the sheets together and continue your line. I recommend using pencil for ease of editing. Begin chronologically or start with your most significant losses and work from there. These will come into your thoughts quickly. As you focus, other events and life changes will begin to surface. If it comes to mind, put it down.

Be prepared for feelings to rise as you do this exercise. If you've experienced multiple losses, you may want to do this work in different sittings. This allows you a chance to spend time with those feelings to honor them. Keep your journal nearby as you work on your timeline. Writing these memories and feelings down as they emerge can be another step in penning your grief story.

My grief stories

What was your first memory of death or another loss?

My daddy

As you read this, think about your first major loss. Pay attention to your feelings. Does any of my story leave you angry or bring tears to your eyes? Any unexpected feelings? As always, keep your journal nearby.

Anger. We all have reasons. What is yours? Who are you angry at for dying, or leaving, or getting sick? Who should still be here?

When you get the chance to say good-bye

How did this impact your grief?

Reproductive Loss

If you've experienced any reproductive loss, please take time to honor that loss, that tiny person, that dream, that hole in your heart. I understand this is a difficult request, but I'd like you to open your journal and write a letter to your baby or babies not with you. Share what you imagined for her, how you felt if you got to hold him, how sorry you are. This is also a chance to face any shame or guilt you might carry – a chance for self-forgiveness. While painful, you'll find this to be a cathartic act of connection and love.

Death by suicide

Have you ever experienced suicidal thoughts or attempted a suicide? Have you gotten help? Are you happy to be alive? Have you had a loved one attempt or complete a suicide? It's important to take a minute and process your feelings. Journal. Make calls if you need to. Write a letter to yourself or a loved one about feelings that have come up.

Loss of self, Retirement, Loss of health

Have you experienced any of these kinds of losses or adjustments in your life? How did you cope? How did you find resolution? Take time for reflection and to make some notes.

When you know you're dying

What have you selected from the fantasy menu of how you get to die? Did that decision comfort you or make you anxious? Have you been with someone who experienced what Hospice would call, a beautiful death? We all have fears. What are yours? Please take some time to think about these questions and write an entry in your journal.

Pet Loss

Don't forget to add significant pet losses to your timeline. And, please, take a few minutes with your journal to tell your story.

Good grief

What thoughts come when you focus on your own transitions? If these transitions created good grief, please take a few minutes to reflect and journal.

National grief

Where were you when? Take a little time to reflect on your memories of these or other national grief events. How did they impact you? Who or what did you lose?

This question is especially relevant during the pandemic. Did a loved one die? Did you lose your health? Were you a frontline worker who still has nightmares? What will you mourn? What did you do different in that first year of isolation? How did the pandemic change your life, your schedule, your connections?

What did you learn? What did you miss that you didn't know you would? Think about these questions scattered throughout this chapter. What stood out for you? What of the questions touched your heart or misted your eyes? What does moving out of this moment in history feel like?

Part IV: Other grief challenges

Holiday grief

Which holiday season had the most meaning in your family story? Where do your early memories lie? Were your holidays happy or clouded by trauma? Making notes now may be helpful in how you experience that holiday in the coming year. You may find by processing feelings that surround your memories, that a healing will begin.

Complicated grief

If any of the topics covered tweak memories of complications in your own grief situations or your family's, take a minute with your journal to honor what feelings come.

When someone a child loves dies

How do you want to talk to your child?

Helping others

How do you want to be there?

Where do we go?

What are your thoughts?

Part V: The toolbox

Basic self-care, attitude, managing symptoms

What do you find helpful?

How we memorialize

Think about your memories and how you've memorialized your special people who have died, and the life changes you've encountered – as you've done throughout this process. How will you keep them present in your heart?

Legacy vision board

Eulogy There were times that I asked you if you had any other suggestions for healing and remembering, or if you've had a loss we didn't talk about. If you have something you'd like to contribute, you can email me at victoriamitchellauthor@gmail.com. Thank you for being a part of this journey.

END NOTES

<u>Introduction</u>

[1]   Joseph Biden. COVID Memorial Speech, Lincoln Memorial Washington D.C., Jan. 19, 2021

[2] Kahlil Gibran, *The Prophet* (New York: Readers Library Classics, 2021), 27

Part I: Our Society and Grief

[3]   Tom Shadyac. Patch Adams. Blue World Productions, 1998. Movie length 1hr, 55min

[4]   Unknown, "Most fears in life trace back to fear of death..."

[5]   Margeret Rinkl, "More and More, I Talk to the Dead" Opinion Guest Essay, New York Times, Jan. 30, 2023

[6]   Pema Chodrin, *How We Live is How We Die* (Boulder: Shambhala Publications, 2022), 11

[7]   Tallu Schuyler Quinn, *What We Wish Were True* (New York: Convergent Books, 2022), 59

[8]   Elizabeth Gilbert. 2018., "Grief does not obey your plans or your wishes...", Instagram, June 6, 2018

[9] Brene' Brown. *Atlas of the Heart*, (New York: Random House, 2021), 104

[10]   1883, Season 1, Episode 10, "This is not Your Heaven" originally aired Feb. 27, 2022

[11]   Emma Payne. "Accessibility and Privilege in Grief Support," Guest essay, Talk Death.com, Aug. 29, 2020

12   Emma Payne. "Accessibility and Privilege in Grief Support," Aug. 29, 2020

Part II: So Much Sadness

13   Ranata Suzuki. 2016. "I never knew." Facebook, Nov. 3, 2016.

14   Joan Didion, *The Year of Magical Thinking*, (New York: Vintage Books, 2005), 27

15   Sherry Walling, PhD. "I'm a Psychologist. After my Brother's Suicide…," Essay, Slate.com, Dec. 4, 2022.

16   Elisabeth Kubler-Ross. (New York: Touchstone, 1997), 51-146-five stages fully explained.

17   Ranata Suzuki. 2016. "It's one of those words." Facebook. Nov. 5, 2016

18   Sherry Walling, PhD. "I'm a Psychologist. After my Brother's Suicide…,"

19   C.S. Lewis, *A Grief Observed*, (New York: Harper Collins, 1961), 20

20   Quinn, *What We Wish Were True,* 135

21   Margaret Renkl. "More and More, I Talk to the Dead," Jan. 30, 2023

22   Jason Isbell and the 400 Unit. "If We Were Vampires" Album: The Nashville Sound, track 5, vinyl, Dave Cobb, producer, 2017

23   Leslie Hill. @lesliechill85, Husband's terminal illness. Instagram

24   Sam Sifton. "Grief and Cooking," Essay, New York Times Cooking, May 28, 2022

[25] Danielle Salmon Deschenes.. @danofish, "I grieve for the years you will miss...", Instagram Aug. 30, 2022

Part III: What We Grieve

[26] Madison Clark, "Sharing Grief," Daily Om online essay, date unknown

[27] Leonard Cohen. "Anthem." Album: The Future, track 4,vinyl, Columbia, 1992

[28] Leo Buscaglia, PhD, *The Fall of Freddy the Leaf* (Thorofare, NJ: SLACK Inc. 1982)

[29] Joan Dideon, *Blue Nights*, (New York: Vintage Books, 2011), 26

[30] Ann Tyler, *Dinner at the Homesick Restaurant,* (New York: Alfred Knopf, Inc. 1982), 4

[31] Saul McLeod, PhD. Erik Erikson's 8 Stages of Psychosocial Development, Simply Psychology online magazine, last updated April 21, 2023. Full explanation of stages.

[32] Abraham Joshua Heschel, *I Asked for Wonder*, (New York: Crossroad Publishing Co., 2013), 88-89

[33] Margareta Magnussen, *The Swedish Art of Aging Exuberantly: Life Wisdom from Someone Who Will (Probably) Die Before You,* (New York: Scribner, 2022), 4

[34] Paul Kalanithi, *When Breath Becomes Air*, (New York: Random House, 2016), 219

[35] Quinn, *What We Wish Were True*, 150

[36] Dacher Keltner, *Awe: The New Science of Everyday Wonder and How It Can Transform Your Life,* (New York: Penguin Press, 2023) 17

37   Unknown, possibly originated @Petfurnitureon Twitter, reposted on Instagram by #lilies abound. Could not find original.

38   The Avett Brothers. "No Hard Feelings." Album: True Sadness, track 3 vinyl, Rick Ruben, producer, 2016

39   Katie Vandenberg. Focus Forward 2022. http//katievandenberg.com/.

40   Holly Peterson. 2020. "My heart hurts so much." Facebook, Dec. 6, 2020.

Part IV: Other Grief Challenges

41   Mitch Albom. *The Five People You Meet in Heaven*, (New York: Hachette Books, 2003) 173

42   Book of Ecclesiastes. *NLV Bible*

43   Leo Buscaglia, PhD, *The Fall of Freddy the Leaf*, 1

44   Pat Schwiebert and Chuck DeKlyen, *Tear Soup* (Portland, OR: Grief Watch, 1999), 4

45   Bryan Mellonie and Robert Ingpen*, Lifetimes: The Beautiful Way to Explain Death to Chidren*, (New York: Bantam Books, 1983), 1

46   C.S. Lewis, *A Grief Observed*, 41

47   Julia Halpert. "How to Help a Loved One Through Sudden Loss." Guest essay, New York Times, Jan. 7, 2022

48 Facebook page, "It's Ok Not to be OK" July 19, 2019

49 Randy Alcorn, *Deadline*, Colorado Springs: (Multnomah Books, 1994), 48-49

50   Anita Moorjani, *Dying to Be Me*, (New York: Hayhouse, 2022), 65-66

51   Kenneth Ring, *Heading Toward Omega*, (New York: William Morrow and Company, 1985), 149

52   Elisabeth Kubler-Ross. *The Wheel of Life,* (New York: Touchstone, 1997), 284

53   Kenneth Ring*, Heading Toward Omega*, 158

54   Brian L. Weiss, M.D., *Many Lives, Many Masters*, (New York: Touchstone, 1988)

Part V: The Toolbox and Other Pieces to Take With You

55   Donna Ashworth, *Loss,* "You May be Gone" (Edinburgh, Scotland: Black and White Publishing, Ltd., 2022), 101

56   Ann Frank*, Diary of a Young Girl,* (New York: Doubleday, 1947), 208

57   Anderson Cooper. 2022. All There Is, Podcast, Episodes 1-7 plus trailer and final chapter, Sept 2, 2022- Nov. 2, 2022.

58   Ellen Barry. "How Long Should it Take to Grieve". Guest essay New York Times, Mar. 18, 2022

59   The Avett Brothers. "No Hard Feelings." 2016

60 Donna Ashworth, *Loss*, "Last Night" 75

61   Heather Brammeier, *The Things We Keep*, sculpture art installation, 2022

62   Max Ehrmann. "Desiderata" first published Michigan Tradesman magazine, April 5, 1933

63 Quinn, *What We Wish Were True,* 185

ACKNOWLEDGMENTS

Thanks to each of you who encouraged me and offered wisdom throughout the writing of *Surviving Grief,* especially during the emotional journey of telling my grief stories.

Thanks to my husband, Marty, always my first reader. I appreciate your input, your sweet notes, your heart, and your tears. And thank you for your computer skills. Thanks to my sons and daughter, daughters-in-law, and son-in-law for cheering me on and pushing when I needed a push – which was often. Thanks to my grandchildren who bring me joy, always. To family and friends, thanks for talking me through fear and hesitance every time I was sure I couldn't do this. Thanks to my readers and contributors. And a shout out to my friend Meg, who performed a needed tough edit.

Thanks to you who vulnerably shared your stories: Leslie Hill, Danielle Salmon Deshenes, Heather Brammeir, Holly Peterson, and ones who chose to be unnamed – your words have inspired me far beyond this writing. And I'm forever grateful to my past clients who allowed me to share their journeys, constantly reminding me of the resilience of the human spirit.

Thanks to David Poyer and Lenore Hart, my publishers at Northampton House Press, for patiently walking me through my plodding work. I also want to acknowledge Tony Morris and Danelle LeJeune at the Ossabaw Island Writer's Retreat, Ossabaw Island, Georgia. I'm grateful for that first step back to writing and the inspiration I found there. And a bow of gratitude to the writers I've cited. I highly recommend every work.

And last, but not least, thanks to you, my readers, for being willing to take this journey to healing, and allowing me to be a part of your sacred act of love.

NORTHAMPTON HOUSE PRESS

Established in 2011, Northampton House Press publishes selected
fiction, nonfiction, and memoir. Check out our list at
www.northampton-house.com, and Like us on Facebook –
"Northampton House Press" – as we showcase more innovative
works from brilliant new talents.

www.ingramcontent.com/pod-product-compliance
Lightning Source LLC
Chambersburg PA
CBHW060922140726
47996CB00001B/348